Managing Database Management with MongoDB, MySQL, and PostgresQL

Modern Database Design and Optimization

Leonardo Conn

COPYRIGHT

Disclaimer

The content presented in this book is for educational and informational purposes only. Every effort has been made to ensure the accuracy of the information at the time of publication; however, the author(s) and publisher make no representations or warranties about the completeness, accuracy, or current applicability of the material provided.

This book may include references to software, hardware, systems, or processes that are subject to change over time. Readers are encouraged to verify the information and ensure compatibility with their specific setups or environments before implementing any of the recommendations, instructions, or code snippets presented. Individual results may vary based on varying hardware, software versions, and user expertise.

The author(s) and publisher assume no liability for any errors, omissions, or outcomes that may arise from the application or use of the information in this book. The implementation of any techniques, processes, or configurations described herein is solely at the reader's own risk. It is recommended that users back up their data and systems and take necessary precautions before making any changes.

For complex technical challenges or if uncertainty arises, consulting with a qualified professional or technical expert is advisable.

Contents

Chapter 1: Introduction to Database Management Systems

Overview of Database Management Systems (DBMS)

Database Management Systems (DBMS) are essential software applications that facilitate the creation, manipulation, management, and retrieval of data in databases. As organizations increasingly rely on data-driven decision-making, the role of DBMS has become pivotal. A DBMS serves as an intermediary between end-users and the database, enabling users to perform operations like storing, retrieving, and managing data efficiently.

At the core of any DBMS is a structured system for organizing data. This structure can vary widely based on the type of database—relational, NoSQL, hierarchical, or object-oriented. In relational databases, data is organized into tables consisting of rows and columns, which makes it easy to manage and query. Conversely, NoSQL databases, such as MongoDB, store data in a more flexible format, such as documents or key-value pairs, allowing for greater scalability and performance in certain applications.

One of the primary functions of a DBMS is to ensure data integrity and consistency. This is particularly crucial in multi-user environments where concurrent access can lead to conflicts. Modern DBMS solutions employ various techniques, such as locking mechanisms and transaction management, to maintain data integrity. The importance of security is also paramount; a DBMS must provide robust access controls and encryption capabilities to protect sensitive data from unauthorized access.

Performance optimization is another critical aspect of DBMS functionality. As data volumes grow, efficient data retrieval becomes increasingly complex. A well-designed DBMS can utilize indexing, caching, and query optimization techniques to ensure that data can be accessed quickly and efficiently. Furthermore, many DBMS solutions offer tools for monitoring performance metrics, which can help administrators identify and resolve bottlenecks.

With the rise of big data and cloud computing, the landscape of database management is evolving rapidly. Traditional relational databases still dominate many applications, but NoSQL databases have gained traction for their ability to handle large volumes of unstructured data. Cloud-based DBMS solutions offer scalability and flexibility, allowing organizations to pay for what they use without investing heavily in on-premises infrastructure.

In summary, DBMS plays a crucial role in modern data management by providing tools for data storage, retrieval, integrity, security, and performance optimization. The choice of DBMS can significantly impact an organization's ability to leverage its data effectively.

Importance of Choosing the Right DBMS

Selecting the appropriate DBMS is a critical decision for any organization, as it directly affects data management, performance, scalability, and long-term sustainability. The choice is not just about technology; it reflects the organization's strategic goals, operational requirements, and growth trajectory. Here are some key factors to consider when evaluating DBMS options:

Data Structure and Complexity

The first consideration is the nature of the data being managed. For instance, if the organization primarily deals with structured data and requires complex relationships among data entities, a relational database like MySQL or PostgreSQL would be a strong candidate. These systems support SQL, which allows for intricate queries and data manipulation. On the other hand, if the data is semi-structured or unstructured, a NoSQL database like MongoDB would offer greater flexibility and ease of use. This distinction is crucial, as the wrong choice can lead to challenges in data management and analysis.

Scalability and Performance Needs

As organizations grow, their data needs often expand exponentially. Therefore, it is essential to choose a DBMS that can scale effectively. Relational databases can scale vertically by enhancing the hardware (e.g., adding more memory or CPU), but they may face limitations when it comes to handling massive volumes of concurrent transactions. NoSQL databases, by contrast, are often designed for horizontal scaling, allowing organizations to distribute data across multiple servers easily. This aspect becomes particularly important in environments where speed and responsiveness are vital, such as in e-commerce or real-time analytics.

Cost Considerations

Cost is a significant factor in DBMS selection. Open-source databases like MySQL and PostgreSQL can be cost-effective options, especially for startups and small businesses, as they eliminate licensing fees. However, organizations must also consider the total cost of ownership, which includes hardware, maintenance, training, and support. In contrast, commercial DBMS solutions may come with high initial costs but often offer robust support and additional features that can justify the investment in the long run.

Community and Support

A strong community or vendor support can make a significant difference in the successful implementation and management of a DBMS. Popular systems like MySQL and PostgreSQL have extensive online communities, forums, and documentation, which can be invaluable for troubleshooting and learning. On the other hand, less popular or niche databases may not have the same level of community support, making it more challenging to resolve issues or find experienced professionals.

Integration Capabilities

In today's interconnected digital landscape, the ability to integrate with other systems is crucial. The chosen DBMS must seamlessly interact with various applications, APIs, and data sources. For instance, if an organization uses cloud-based services, the DBMS should have robust integration capabilities with those platforms. Moreover, support for standard data formats and protocols can enhance interoperability with existing systems.

Security Features

Data breaches and cyber threats are increasingly common, making security a top priority in DBMS selection. The chosen system must offer strong security features, including user authentication, access controls, encryption, and auditing capabilities. Organizations dealing with sensitive data, such as healthcare or finance, may have additional compliance requirements that necessitate stringent security measures.

Future-Proofing

Finally, organizations should consider the future growth and evolution of their data needs. As technology advances, the capabilities of DBMS systems continue to evolve. Choosing a system with a clear development roadmap and regular updates can ensure that the organization remains competitive and can leverage new features as they become available.

In , the importance of choosing the right DBMS cannot be overstated. It affects every aspect of data management and utilization within an organization. By carefully considering the various factors outlined above, organizations can make informed decisions that align their database technology with their strategic objectives.

Comparison of MongoDB, MySQL, and PostgreSQL

As organizations evaluate their database management options, three popular systems often come to the forefront: MongoDB, MySQL, and PostgreSQL. Each of these databases has its unique strengths and weaknesses, making them suitable for different use cases and operational needs.

MongoDB

MongoDB is a NoSQL document-oriented database that uses a flexible schema, allowing for the storage of unstructured and semi-structured data. This flexibility makes MongoDB an excellent choice for applications that require rapid development and adaptability, such as content management systems, real-time analytics, and Internet of Things (IoT) applications.

Key Features of MongoDB

Schema Flexibility: MongoDB allows developers to create data structures that can evolve over time without requiring major changes to the underlying schema. This is particularly useful for applications that undergo frequent updates or changes in data requirements.

Scalability: MongoDB supports horizontal scaling through sharding, which enables the distribution of data across multiple servers. This feature allows organizations to handle large volumes of data and user traffic seamlessly.

Rich Query Language: MongoDB offers a powerful query language that supports complex queries, aggregations, and indexing, enabling developers to retrieve data efficiently.

High Availability: Through replica sets, MongoDB ensures that data is highly available, providing automatic failover and data redundancy.

MySQL

MySQL is one of the most widely used relational database management systems (RDBMS) in the world. It operates under a structured schema and uses SQL (Structured Query Language) for data manipulation. MySQL is particularly popular among web applications and businesses that require high reliability and data integrity.

Key Features of MySQL

ACID Compliance: MySQL is known for its adherence to ACID (Atomicity, Consistency, Isolation, Durability) principles, making it a reliable choice for transactional applications, such as financial systems and e-commerce platforms.

Robust Security Features: MySQL offers strong security mechanisms, including user management, role-based access controls, and data encryption, ensuring that sensitive information is well protected.

Performance Optimization: MySQL provides a range of optimization features, including indexing, query caching, and partitioning, which enhance performance, especially in read-heavy environments.

Strong Community and Ecosystem: MySQL has a large and active community, offering extensive resources, documentation, and third-party tools that enhance its functionality.

PostgreSQL

PostgreSQL is another leading open-source relational database that excels in handling complex queries and large datasets. Known for its advanced features and compliance with SQL standards, PostgreSQL is suitable for a wide range of applications, from web services to data warehousing.

Key Features of PostgreSQL

Advanced Data Types: PostgreSQL supports a wide variety of data types, including JSON, XML, and user-defined types, making it versatile for different data models.

Extensibility: One of the standout features of PostgreSQL is its extensibility. Users can create custom functions, operators, and data types, allowing for tailored solutions that meet specific needs.

Strong Concurrency Control: PostgreSQL uses Multi-Version Concurrency Control (MVCC) to handle multiple transactions simultaneously without locking, improving performance in high-traffic environments.

Geospatial Data Support: With the PostGIS extension, PostgreSQL excels in managing geospatial data, making it a popular choice for applications that involve mapping and location services.

Summary of Comparisons

In summary, MongoDB, MySQL, and PostgreSQL each serve distinct purposes and have unique features that cater to different organizational needs. While MongoDB offers flexibility and scalability for unstructured data, MySQL is a reliable choice for transactional applications requiring strong consistency and data integrity. PostgreSQL stands out with its

Chapter 2: Understanding NoSQL vs. SQL Databases

Definition and Characteristics of NoSQL Databases

NoSQL databases emerged as a response to the limitations of traditional relational database management systems (RDBMS) in handling the growing demands of modern applications. The term "NoSQL" is somewhat of a misnomer, as it does not strictly mean "no SQL." Rather, it encompasses a diverse category of databases that are designed to handle various types of data, including unstructured and semi-structured formats, without adhering to the rigid schemas associated with relational databases.

Key Characteristics of NoSQL Databases

Schema Flexibility: Unlike relational databases, which require a predefined schema, NoSQL databases allow for dynamic schemas. This means that data can be stored in various formats, and new fields can be added without disrupting existing data. This flexibility is particularly beneficial for applications that evolve rapidly, such as web services and mobile applications.

Horizontal Scalability: NoSQL databases are designed to scale out rather than up. This means that instead of relying on more powerful hardware (vertical scaling), they can distribute data across multiple servers (horizontal scaling). This architecture allows organizations to manage large volumes of data and accommodate increased user traffic seamlessly.

Variety of Data Models: NoSQL databases encompass several data models, including key-value stores, document stores, column-family stores, and graph databases. Each model is optimized for specific use cases, enabling developers to choose the best fit for their applications. For instance, document stores like MongoDB excel in managing JSON-like documents, while graph databases like Neo4j are ideal for applications that involve complex relationships.

Eventual Consistency: Many NoSQL databases prioritize availability and partition tolerance over immediate consistency, adopting an eventual consistency model. This means that while data may not be immediately consistent across all nodes, it will become consistent over time. This trade-off is often acceptable for applications where high availability is crucial, such as social media platforms.

Performance Optimization for Read and Write Operations: NoSQL databases are typically optimized for high performance in read and write operations. This is achieved through techniques such as data partitioning and in-memory storage, which enable quick data retrieval and processing.

Open-Source Options: Many NoSQL databases are available as open-source projects, allowing organizations to implement and customize them without the licensing costs associated with proprietary solutions. This has led to widespread adoption, particularly among startups and technology companies.

In summary, NoSQL databases are characterized by their schema flexibility, horizontal scalability, variety of data models, eventual consistency, performance optimization, and open-source availability. These features make NoSQL an attractive choice for modern applications that require agility, scalability, and performance.

SQL Database Fundamentals

Structured Query Language (SQL) databases are the cornerstone of traditional data management systems. SQL databases are designed to store structured data in a tabular format, consisting of rows and columns. This relational model is based on a set of mathematical principles that provide a solid foundation for data organization and retrieval.

Key Features of SQL Databases

Structured Data Storage: SQL databases require a predefined schema, which defines the structure of the data, including tables, fields, and relationships between tables. This strict structure ensures data integrity and consistency, making SQL databases suitable for applications where data relationships are critical, such as financial systems and enterprise resource planning (ERP) software.

ACID Compliance: SQL databases are known for their adherence to ACID properties—Atomicity, Consistency, Isolation, and Durability. These properties ensure that database transactions are processed reliably, maintaining data integrity even in the face of failures. For example, in a banking application, a funds transfer must either be fully completed or fully rolled back to avoid inconsistencies.

Powerful Query Capabilities: SQL provides a rich query language that allows users to perform complex queries and data manipulation. With SQL, users can join multiple tables, aggregate data, filter results, and sort data efficiently. This powerful querying capability is one of the primary reasons for the enduring popularity of SQL databases.

Data Integrity and Constraints: SQL databases enforce data integrity through constraints such as primary keys, foreign keys, unique constraints, and check constraints. These mechanisms ensure that data adheres to predefined rules, preventing invalid data entries and maintaining consistency across related tables.

Transaction Management: SQL databases support transaction management, allowing multiple operations to be bundled into a single transaction. This ensures that either all operations succeed or none do, providing a reliable mechanism for maintaining data integrity during concurrent operations.

Extensive Ecosystem and Tools: SQL databases have a long history, resulting in a rich ecosystem of tools, libraries, and frameworks. This extensive support makes it easier for developers to integrate SQL databases into applications and manage them effectively.

In summary, SQL databases are characterized by their structured data storage, ACID compliance, powerful query capabilities, data integrity mechanisms, transaction management, and a robust ecosystem. These features make SQL databases a reliable choice for applications that require strict data organization and integrity.

When to Use NoSQL vs. SQL

The decision to use a NoSQL or SQL database depends on various factors, including the specific requirements of the application, data structure, scalability needs, and performance considerations. Understanding the strengths and weaknesses of each type of database is crucial for making an informed decision.

When to Use NoSQL Databases

Handling Unstructured or Semi-Structured Data: NoSQL databases are ideal for applications that deal with unstructured or semi-structured data, such as social media posts, multimedia content, and IoT sensor data. Their flexible schema allows for diverse data types, making them suitable for rapidly evolving applications.

Rapid Development and Agile Methodologies: In environments where speed is crucial, NoSQL databases enable rapid development cycles. Developers can make changes to the data model without complex migrations, allowing teams to iterate quickly and respond to changing business needs.

Large Volumes of Data: If the application is expected to generate massive amounts of data, such as logs, user interactions, or sensor readings, NoSQL databases provide the necessary scalability. Their ability to scale horizontally allows organizations to distribute data across multiple nodes, ensuring that performance remains high even as data volumes grow.

High Availability Requirements: Applications that demand high availability, such as e-commerce platforms and real-time analytics, can benefit from NoSQL's eventual consistency model. This approach allows for system resilience, even in the face of network partitions.

Flexible Querying Needs: If the application requires flexible querying capabilities that can change over time, NoSQL databases are well-suited for the task. Their ability to support diverse query patterns allows for adaptability as application requirements evolve.

When to Use SQL Databases

Structured Data with Defined Relationships: SQL databases are best suited for applications that require structured data storage with well-defined relationships between entities. For instance, financial applications, inventory management systems, and customer relationship management (CRM) software often rely on the relational model to enforce data integrity.

Transactional Systems: If the application demands strong transactional capabilities, SQL databases are the preferred choice. Their ACID compliance ensures that complex transactions are processed reliably, making them ideal for scenarios such as online banking and reservation systems.

Data Integrity and Consistency: When maintaining data integrity and consistency is paramount, SQL databases provide robust mechanisms for enforcing rules and constraints. This makes them suitable for applications that require strict adherence to data quality standards.

Complex Querying and Reporting: Applications that require complex querying, aggregations, and reporting often benefit from the powerful querying capabilities of SQL. SQL databases allow users to perform sophisticated queries and generate detailed reports, making them suitable for data analysis and business intelligence applications.

Legacy Systems and Integration: In organizations with established legacy systems that rely on SQL databases, it may be more practical to continue using SQL due to compatibility and integration considerations. Migrating to a different database system can be resource-intensive and risky.

In , the choice between NoSQL and SQL databases hinges on various factors, including data structure, application requirements, scalability needs, and performance considerations. By carefully evaluating these aspects, organizations can select the most suitable database technology to meet their specific goals and challenges.

Chapter 3: Setting Up Your Database Environment

Installation and Configuration of MongoDB

Setting up MongoDB involves a series of steps, from installation to configuration. This section will guide you through the process of getting MongoDB up and running, whether on a local machine or in a cloud environment.

System Requirements

Before installation, ensure that your system meets the necessary requirements. MongoDB supports various operating systems, including Windows, macOS, and Linux. Check the official MongoDB documentation for the latest version and its requirements, which typically include:

A supported OS (Windows 10, macOS, or specific Linux distributions)
A minimum of 2GB of RAM (4GB or more recommended)
Disk space based on expected data size

Downloading MongoDB

To download MongoDB, follow these steps:

Visit the MongoDB Download Center.

Select the appropriate version for your operating system.

Choose the package type (MSI for Windows, TAR for Linux, or DMG for macOS).

Download the installer.

Installation Steps

Windows Installation

Run the Installer: Double-click the downloaded MSI file. The setup wizard will guide you through the installation process.

Select Setup Type: Choose between "Complete" or "Custom." The complete option installs all components.

Service Configuration: During installation, configure MongoDB to run as a Windows service. This ensures MongoDB starts automatically with your system.

Finish Installation: Click "Install" to begin the process. Once completed, MongoDB will be installed on your system.

Linux Installation

Use Package Manager: Open a terminal and use a package manager to install MongoDB. For example, on Ubuntu, you would run:

bash

Copy code

```
sudo apt-get install -y mongodb
```

Start MongoDB Service: After installation, start the MongoDB service with:

bash

Copy code

```
sudo service mongodb start
```

Enable Auto-Start: To ensure MongoDB starts automatically on boot, use:

bash

Copy code

```
sudo systemctl enable mongodb
```

macOS Installation

Use Homebrew: If you have Homebrew installed, you can install MongoDB easily:

bash

Copy code

```
brew tap mongodb/brew
brew install mongodb-community
```

Start MongoDB: Start the MongoDB service using:

bash

Copy code

```
brew services start mongodb-community
```

Configuration

After installation, you may want to configure MongoDB settings. The default configuration file is usually located at `/etc/mongod.conf` on Linux or `C:\Program Files\MongoDB\Server\<version>\bin\mongod.cfg` on Windows. Here are some common configuration options:

Data Directory: Specify where MongoDB should store its data files.
yaml
Copy code

```
storage:
dbPath: /var/lib/mongodb
```

Network Interfaces: Define which IP addresses MongoDB should listen on.
yaml
Copy code

```
net:
```

```
bindIp: 127.0.0.1    # Allows only local
connections
port: 27017
```

Authorization: Enable authorization for security.
yaml
Copy code
```
security:
authorization: enabled
```

After making changes to the configuration file, restart the MongoDB service for the changes to take effect.

Verifying the Installation

To ensure that MongoDB is installed correctly, you can use the MongoDB shell. Open a terminal or command prompt and type:

bash
Copy code
```
mongo
```

If the installation is successful, you will enter the MongoDB shell, where you can begin interacting with your database.

Installing MySQL

Setting up MySQL involves similar steps to MongoDB, but with specific considerations unique to relational database systems. Here's how to install and configure MySQL.

System Requirements

Before installation, ensure your system meets MySQL's requirements. These generally include:

Supported operating systems (Windows, macOS, Linux)
At least 2GB of RAM (4GB or more recommended)
Sufficient disk space for data storage

Downloading MySQL

You can download MySQL from the official MySQL website:

Visit the MySQL Community Downloads.
Choose your operating system and select the version you wish to install.
Download the installer package.

Installation Steps

Windows Installation

Run the Installer: Open the downloaded installer. Choose between the Developer Default or Server Only options based on your needs.

Configuration Steps: Follow the configuration wizard to set up the root password and configure server settings.

Install MySQL as a Service: Choose to run MySQL as a Windows service. You can also choose to start it automatically.

Linux Installation

Using Package Manager: On Ubuntu, for example, run:
bash
Copy code

```bash
sudo apt-get install mysql-server
```

Secure Installation: After installation, run the security script:
bash
Copy code

```bash
sudo mysql_secure_installation
```

This script will prompt you to set the root password and remove anonymous users.

Start MySQL Service: Use:
bash
Copy code

```bash
sudo service mysql start
```

macOS Installation

Using Homebrew: If you have Homebrew installed, you can install MySQL with:

bash

Copy code

```
brew install mysql
```

Start MySQL Service: Use:

bash

Copy code

```
brew services start mysql
```

Configuration

MySQL's configuration file, `my.cnf`, is typically located in `/etc/mysql/` on Linux or `C:\ProgramData\MySQL\MySQL Server <version>\my.ini` on Windows. Common settings include:

Data Directory: Define where MySQL will store its data files.

ini

Copy code

```
[mysqld]
```

```
datadir=/var/lib/mysql
```

Bind Address: Set which IP addresses MySQL will listen to.
ini
Copy code
```
bind-address = 127.0.0.1
```

Character Set: Define the default character set and collation.
ini
Copy code
```
character-set-server=utf8mb4
collation-server=utf8mb4_unicode_ci
```

After making any changes, restart the MySQL service.

Verifying the Installation

To verify that MySQL is running correctly, log in to the MySQL shell with:

bash
Copy code
```
mysql -u root -p
```

Enter your root password when prompted. If successful, you will enter the MySQL shell and can begin managing your databases.

Installing PostgreSQL

PostgreSQL is known for its robustness and advanced features. Setting it up involves several key steps.

System Requirements

Ensure your system meets the minimum requirements:

Supported operating systems (Windows, macOS, Linux)
At least 1GB of RAM (more for larger databases)
Sufficient disk space for data storage

Downloading PostgreSQL

You can download PostgreSQL from the official PostgreSQL website:

Visit the PostgreSQL Downloads page.
Choose your operating system and follow the instructions to download the installer.

Installation Steps

Windows Installation

Run the Installer: Open the downloaded executable. Follow the installation wizard steps.

Choose Components: Select the components to install (server, pgAdmin, command-line tools).

Set the Password: During installation, set the password for the PostgreSQL superuser (default user is `postgres`).

Finish Installation: Complete the installation and optionally configure PostgreSQL as a Windows service.

Linux Installation

Using Package Manager: On Ubuntu, run:

bash

Copy code

```
sudo apt-get install postgresql postgresql-contrib
```

Start PostgreSQL Service: Use:

bash

Copy code

```
sudo service postgresql start
```

macOS Installation

Using Homebrew: Install PostgreSQL with:
bash
Copy code

```
brew install postgresql
```

Start PostgreSQL Service: Use:
bash
Copy code

```
brew services start postgresql
```

Configuration

PostgreSQL's configuration files are typically located in `/etc/postgresql/<version>/main/` on Linux or in the PostgreSQL installation directory on Windows. Important configurations include:

Data Directory: Define where PostgreSQL will store its data files.
conf
Copy code

```
data_directory                         =
'/var/lib/postgresql/<version>/main'
```

Listening Addresses: Set which IP addresses PostgreSQL will accept connections from.
conf
Copy code

```
listen_addresses = 'localhost'
```

Authentication Methods: Configure user authentication methods, usually found in the `pg_hba.conf` file.

Verifying the Installation

To verify that PostgreSQL is functioning correctly, you can log in to the PostgreSQL shell with:

bash
Copy code

```
psql -U postgres
```

You will be prompted for the password you set during installation. Upon successful login, you can start managing your databases.

Setting Up Development Environments and Tools

Once the databases are installed, setting up a suitable development environment is essential for effective database management and application development.

Chapter 4: Designing Your Database Schema

Understanding Database Schema

A database schema is a blueprint that outlines how data is organized within a database. It defines the structure of the database, including tables, fields, relationships, and constraints. A well-designed schema is crucial for ensuring data integrity, optimizing performance, and facilitating efficient data retrieval. The design process involves several steps, from understanding data requirements to creating the physical schema in a specific database management system.

Types of Database Schemas

There are several types of schemas to consider during the design process:

Conceptual Schema: This high-level representation outlines what data will be stored and how it will relate to other data without detailing how it will be implemented physically. It serves as a foundation for further design.

Logical Schema: This schema provides a more detailed view, including specific data types, constraints, and relationships among data entities. It translates the conceptual schema into a structure that can be implemented in a database.

Physical Schema: This schema describes how data is physically stored in the database. It includes details about file organization, indexing methods, and storage allocation. This level of detail is crucial for performance optimization and maintenance.

Understanding these different schema types helps database designers create a comprehensive plan that covers all aspects of data organization.

Identifying Requirements

Before designing the schema, it is essential to gather requirements from stakeholders. This process typically involves:

Interviews: Engage with end-users, business analysts, and other stakeholders to understand their data needs and how they interact with the system.
Use Cases: Define use cases that illustrate how users will interact with the database. This helps identify the data entities, relationships, and access patterns.
Data Analysis: Analyze existing data, if available, to understand its structure, volume, and quality. This analysis can provide insights into potential challenges and opportunities.

This requirements-gathering phase is critical to ensure that the schema design aligns with user needs and business objectives.

Entity-Relationship (ER) Modeling

An Entity-Relationship (ER) model is a visual representation of the data requirements and relationships within a database. It serves as a crucial step in the schema design process, providing a clear overview of how entities (data objects) relate to one another.

Entities and Attributes

In ER modeling, entities represent distinct objects or concepts in the domain being modeled. For example, in an e-commerce application, entities might include `Customer`, `Product`, and `Order`. Each entity has attributes that define its properties. For instance, a `Customer` entity may have attributes like `CustomerID`, `Name`, `Email`, and `Address`.

Relationships

Relationships define how entities interact with one another. There are three primary types of relationships in ER modeling:

One-to-One (1:1): Each instance of one entity relates to one instance of another. For example, each `Employee` might have one `EmployeeID`.

One-to-Many (1
): An instance of one entity can relate to multiple instances of another. For instance, a `Customer` can have multiple `Orders`.

Many-to-Many (M
): Instances of one entity can relate to multiple instances of

another. For example, a `Product` can appear in multiple `Orders`, and each `Order` can include multiple `Products`. This relationship often requires a junction table to implement in a relational database.

Creating the ER Diagram

An ER diagram visually represents the entities, attributes, and relationships. It typically includes:

Entities: Represented by rectangles, with attributes listed inside or connected with lines.
Relationships: Depicted as diamonds or lines connecting entities, annotated with cardinality (1:1, 1
, M
).
Primary Keys: Underlined attributes that uniquely identify an entity instance.
Foreign Keys: Attributes that establish relationships between entities.

The ER diagram serves as a blueprint for creating the logical schema and aids in discussions with stakeholders.

Normalization and Denormalization

Normalization is the process of organizing data in a way that reduces redundancy and dependency. It involves dividing large tables into smaller, related ones and defining relationships between them. Denormalization, on the other hand, is the deliberate introduction of redundancy into a database to optimize read performance.

Normalization Forms

Normalization typically follows several stages, known as normal forms. The most common forms include:

First Normal Form (1NF): Requires that all attributes in a table contain only atomic values (no repeating groups or arrays). Each entry in a column must be of the same data type.
Second Normal Form (2NF): Builds on 1NF by ensuring that all non-key attributes are fully functionally dependent on the primary key. This eliminates partial dependencies.
Third Normal Form (3NF): Builds on 2NF by ensuring that no transitive dependencies exist. Non-key attributes must not depend on other non-key attributes.

Normalization helps to eliminate data anomalies and maintain data integrity, but it can also complicate queries and degrade performance in some cases.

When to Denormalize

While normalization is essential, there are scenarios where denormalization may be beneficial:

Performance Optimization: In read-heavy applications where performance is critical, denormalization can reduce the number of joins required in queries, speeding up data retrieval.

Simplified Queries: Denormalized structures can simplify complex queries, making it easier for developers to access the data they need without extensive JOIN operations.

Caching Strategies: Denormalization can work well in conjunction with caching strategies, where frequently accessed data is stored in a more accessible format.

However, denormalization introduces redundancy and can lead to data inconsistencies if not managed carefully. It's crucial to strike a balance between normalization and denormalization based on application requirements.

Physical Implementation

Once the schema design is complete, it's time to implement it in the chosen database management system. This process involves translating the logical schema into the physical schema.

Creating Tables and Relationships

Using the SQL commands, you will create tables based on the defined entities, specifying data types for each attribute and setting primary and foreign keys. For example, creating a Customer table might look like this:

sql
Copy code

```sql
CREATE TABLE Customer (
CustomerID INT PRIMARY KEY,
Name VARCHAR(255),
Email VARCHAR(255),
Address TEXT
);
```

To establish a one-to-many relationship between Customer and Order, you would create the Order table with a foreign key reference:

sql
Copy code

```sql
CREATE TABLE Order (
OrderID INT PRIMARY KEY,
OrderDate DATE,
CustomerID INT,
FOREIGN KEY (CustomerID) REFERENCES Customer(CustomerID)
);
```

Indexing for Performance

Indexes are crucial for optimizing query performance. Creating indexes on frequently queried fields can significantly speed up data retrieval. For example:

sql
Copy code
```
CREATE INDEX idx_customer_email ON Customer
(Email);
```

However, it's essential to balance indexing, as too many indexes can slow down write operations.

Implementing Constraints

Enforce data integrity by implementing constraints such as NOT NULL, UNIQUE, and CHECK constraints. These constraints help ensure that the data adheres to business rules and requirements.

Testing the Schema

Before deploying the database schema into production, thorough testing is necessary. This includes:

Unit Testing: Validate individual components, such as triggers and stored procedures, to ensure they function correctly.
Load Testing: Simulate real-world usage to evaluate how the database performs under load and identify potential bottlenecks.

User Acceptance Testing (UAT): Involve end-users to ensure the schema meets their needs and expectations.

Documentation

Finally, comprehensive documentation of the database schema is essential for ongoing maintenance and future development. Documentation should include:

Schema Diagrams: Visual representations of the schema, including ER diagrams and table structures.
Data Dictionary: A detailed description of each table, including its purpose, attributes, data types, and constraints.
Change Logs: Keep records of changes made to the schema over time, including reasons for modifications and impact assessments.

Well-documented schemas facilitate collaboration among team members and help new developers understand the database structure quickly.

In , designing a database schema involves a careful balance of requirements gathering, modeling, normalization, implementation, and documentation. By following these best practices, you can create a robust, efficient, and maintainable database structure that meets your organization's needs.

Chapter 5: Data Modeling Techniques

Introduction to Data Modeling

Data modeling is a critical process in database design that involves creating a conceptual representation of data structures and their relationships. It serves as a blueprint for building the database and ensures that the data is organized, consistent, and aligned with business needs. Effective data modeling helps in understanding the data requirements, facilitates communication among stakeholders, and lays the groundwork for efficient database implementation.

Importance of Data Modeling

Data modeling provides numerous benefits, including:

Improved Communication: By visualizing data structures, stakeholders—such as business analysts, developers, and end-users—can better understand how data is organized and how it relates to business processes.

Enhanced Data Quality: A well-structured data model helps enforce data integrity and consistency, reducing the chances of anomalies and errors in the data.

Efficient Database Design: Data models help identify redundancies and design relationships, leading to more efficient database schemas that optimize performance and storage.

Scalability and Flexibility: A clear data model allows for easier updates and modifications, ensuring that the database can grow and adapt to changing business requirements.

Types of Data Models

There are several types of data models, each serving different purposes and levels of abstraction. Understanding these models is essential for selecting the right approach for your database design.

Conceptual Data Model

The conceptual data model provides a high-level view of the data requirements without delving into implementation details. It focuses on identifying the main entities and their relationships, serving as a foundation for further modeling. Key features include:

Entities: Major objects or concepts in the domain (e.g., `Customer`, `Product`, `Order`).

Relationships: Associations between entities (e.g., a `Customer` places an `Order`).

Attributes: Essential characteristics of each entity, although detailed attributes may not be included in this model.

Conceptual models are often created using Entity-Relationship (ER) diagrams or Unified Modeling Language (UML) diagrams. They facilitate discussions among stakeholders and help clarify data requirements.

Logical Data Model

The logical data model builds upon the conceptual model by adding more details about the data structure. It defines the specific attributes, data types, and relationships among entities without specifying how the data will be physically implemented. Key aspects include:

Attributes: Detailed definitions of each entity's properties, including data types (e.g., VARCHAR, INT) and constraints (e.g., NOT NULL, UNIQUE).
Primary and Foreign Keys: Identification of primary keys that uniquely identify records and foreign keys that establish relationships between tables.
Normalization: Ensuring that the model adheres to normalization principles, eliminating redundancy and dependencies.

Logical models are crucial for understanding how data will be structured and accessed, guiding the physical implementation phase.

Physical Data Model

The physical data model translates the logical data model into a specific database management system (DBMS) implementation. It incorporates details such as storage structures, indexing strategies, and performance optimization. Key components include:

Table Structures: Definitions of how each entity will be represented as a table in the database, including columns, data types, and constraints.
Indexes: Specifications for indexes to improve query performance, including which columns to index based on access patterns.
Partitioning and Sharding: Strategies for distributing data across multiple storage locations for scalability and performance.

The physical data model is essential for translating design decisions into actionable database structures that can be deployed in a DBMS.

Data Modeling Techniques

Different techniques can be employed for data modeling, each with its strengths and use cases. Here are some commonly used techniques:

Entity-Relationship Modeling (ER Modeling)

Entity-Relationship modeling is one of the most widely used techniques for data modeling. It involves creating ER diagrams that depict entities, attributes, and relationships. Key elements include:

Entities: Represented by rectangles, they denote real-world objects or concepts.
Attributes: Listed within the entity rectangle or connected by ovals, they describe the properties of the entity.
Relationships: Depicted as diamonds or lines connecting entities, annotated with cardinality (e.g., 1:1, 1
, M
) to illustrate how entities interact.

ER modeling is intuitive and visually communicates complex relationships, making it suitable for collaborative design processes.

Unified Modeling Language (UML)

UML is a standardized modeling language that provides various diagram types for software design, including data modeling. UML class diagrams can represent data structures, attributes, and relationships in a way similar to ER diagrams. Key features include:

Classes: Represented by rectangles, similar to entities in ER diagrams.

Attributes: Listed within the class rectangle, detailing the properties of the class.

Associations: Lines connecting classes, indicating relationships and their multiplicity.

UML is particularly useful in environments where software design and data modeling need to be integrated, providing a unified approach.

Star Schema and Snowflake Schema

Star and snowflake schemas are popular techniques for organizing data in data warehousing and business intelligence contexts. They focus on optimizing query performance and simplifying data retrieval.

Star Schema: A star schema consists of a central fact table connected to multiple dimension tables. The fact table contains quantitative data (e.g., sales amounts), while dimension tables provide context (e.g., product details, customer demographics). This structure is intuitive and allows for efficient querying.

Snowflake Schema: A snowflake schema is a more normalized version of a star schema, where dimension tables are further divided into related tables. For example, a `Product` dimension might be split into `Category` and `Subcategory` tables. While this structure reduces redundancy, it can complicate queries due to additional joins.

Both schemas serve specific purposes in analytical environments, with star schemas generally favored for simplicity and performance.

Dimensional Modeling

Dimensional modeling is a technique specifically designed for data warehousing and analytics. It focuses on creating a data structure that is intuitive for end-users and optimized for query performance. Key components include:

Facts: Numeric data that represent business metrics (e.g., sales revenue, transaction counts).
Dimensions: Descriptive attributes related to facts, providing context for analysis (e.g., time, location, product).
Fact Tables and Dimension Tables: Fact tables store quantitative data, while dimension tables store contextual information. The relationship between fact and dimension tables allows for rich analytical queries.

Dimensional modeling is widely used in building data warehouses and analytical systems, enabling effective reporting and business intelligence.

Best Practices for Data Modeling

To ensure effective data modeling, consider the following best practices:

Engage Stakeholders

Involve relevant stakeholders throughout the data modeling process. Regularly gather feedback to ensure that the model aligns with business requirements and user needs. Engaging users can help uncover hidden requirements and improve the overall design.

Use Standard Notation

Adopt standard notation for data modeling, such as ER diagrams or UML. Consistency in notation helps communicate designs effectively and makes it easier for team members to understand the model.

Iterate and Refine

Data modeling is an iterative process. Start with a high-level model and refine it as you gather more information. Be open to revisiting and revising the model based on feedback and changing requirements.

Document Everything

Thoroughly document the data model, including descriptions of entities, attributes, relationships, and constraints. This documentation serves as a reference for developers and analysts and ensures that the model can be maintained and updated in the future.

Consider Performance

Design the data model with performance in mind. Consider how data will be accessed, the types of queries that will be executed, and potential indexing strategies to optimize retrieval. Balancing normalization and denormalization based on access patterns can enhance performance.

Plan for Future Growth

Anticipate future changes and growth in data requirements. Design the model to be flexible and scalable, allowing for easy modifications as the business evolves. Consider potential new data sources and how they might fit into the existing model.

Data modeling is a foundational step in database design that significantly impacts the effectiveness of data storage and retrieval. By employing appropriate modeling techniques, engaging stakeholders, and following best practices, organizations can create robust data models that meet current needs and adapt to future changes. Effective data modeling not only enhances data quality but also fosters better communication and collaboration among teams, ultimately contributing to successful data-driven decision-making.

Chapter 6: Optimizing Database Performance

Introduction to Database Performance Optimization

Database performance optimization is a critical aspect of database management that focuses on enhancing the efficiency of data retrieval, storage, and processing. A well-optimized database can handle large volumes of data and concurrent user requests without compromising performance. As applications grow in complexity and data size, optimizing database performance becomes essential to ensure a smooth user experience and reliable application functionality.

Importance of Database Performance Optimization

Optimizing database performance is vital for several reasons:

User Experience: Slow database performance can lead to delayed responses in applications, negatively affecting user satisfaction. Fast data retrieval and processing are crucial for maintaining a seamless user experience.

Scalability: As the volume of data and the number of users increase, a well-optimized database can scale more effectively. Performance optimization strategies ensure that the database can handle growth without degradation in performance.

Cost Efficiency: Improved performance can lead to cost savings, as optimized databases require fewer resources to manage. Efficient use of storage and processing power can reduce operational costs.

System Reliability: A well-optimized database can reduce the risk of system crashes and downtime, ensuring that applications remain available to users.

Performance Metrics

To effectively optimize database performance, it's essential to understand key performance metrics. These metrics provide insights into how well the database is functioning and where improvements can be made.

Response Time

Response time measures the time taken for the database to execute a query and return results. A high response time indicates potential performance issues. Monitoring response time helps identify slow queries and optimize them.

Throughput

Throughput refers to the number of transactions or queries the database can handle in a given time frame. It is typically measured in transactions per second (TPS) or queries per second

(QPS). Higher throughput indicates better performance and capacity to handle concurrent users.

Latency

Latency measures the delay between a request and the response. It includes network latency and processing time within the database. Reducing latency is crucial for improving overall performance.

CPU Utilization

CPU utilization indicates how much of the database server's processing power is being used. High CPU usage can signal performance bottlenecks, often caused by inefficient queries or inadequate indexing.

I/O Operations

I/O operations measure the number of read and write operations performed on the database storage. Monitoring I/O performance helps identify slow disk access and potential bottlenecks in data retrieval.

Memory Usage

Memory usage metrics indicate how much memory is allocated to the database for caching and processing. Insufficient memory can lead to increased disk I/O and slower performance.

By regularly monitoring these metrics, database administrators (DBAs) can identify areas that require optimization and track the effectiveness of performance improvement strategies.

Query Optimization

One of the most significant factors affecting database performance is the efficiency of SQL queries. Optimizing queries can drastically improve response times and reduce resource consumption.

Indexing

Indexes are critical for improving query performance by allowing the database to quickly locate and retrieve data. However, they come with overhead during data modifications. Here are key considerations for indexing:

Choose the Right Columns: Index columns that are frequently used in WHERE clauses, JOIN conditions, and ORDER BY clauses. Avoid indexing columns with low cardinality, such as boolean values.

Composite Indexes: When queries filter on multiple columns, consider creating composite indexes. A composite index on (column1, column2) can significantly enhance performance for queries that filter by both columns.

Maintain Indexes: Regularly monitor and rebuild indexes to ensure they remain effective. Fragmented indexes can slow down queries and should be re-evaluated periodically.

Query Execution Plans

Analyzing query execution plans provides insights into how the database executes a query. This analysis helps identify inefficient operations and potential improvements. Key aspects to consider include:

Join Methods: Understanding whether the database uses nested loops, hash joins, or merge joins can indicate performance issues. Choosing the right join method can significantly impact query execution time.

Table Scans vs. Index Scans: A table scan occurs when the database reads the entire table to fulfill a query, while an index scan utilizes an index to retrieve only the necessary data. Optimizing queries to leverage indexes can reduce execution time.

Avoiding Subqueries

In some cases, replacing subqueries with JOINs can improve performance. Subqueries can lead to inefficient execution plans, while JOINs often allow the database to optimize data retrieval more effectively. Evaluate the execution plans of both approaches to determine the best option.

Limit Returned Data

Reducing the amount of data returned by queries can improve performance. Use SELECT statements to specify only the columns needed rather than using SELECT *. Additionally, implement pagination techniques to limit the number of rows returned in a single query.

Batch Processing

For operations that involve inserting or updating multiple rows, consider using batch processing. Executing multiple operations in a single transaction reduces the overhead associated with individual queries and can significantly improve performance.

Database Configuration Tuning

Database configuration plays a vital role in overall performance. Tuning various configuration parameters can enhance the efficiency of database operations.

Memory Allocation

Adjusting memory settings can have a significant impact on performance. Key parameters to consider include:

Buffer Pool Size: The buffer pool is used to cache data pages. Increasing its size can reduce disk I/O and improve read performance.

Sort Memory: Allocating adequate memory for sorting operations can speed up query execution, particularly for queries that involve ORDER BY clauses.

Connection Pooling: Configure connection pooling to manage database connections efficiently. Connection pooling reduces the overhead of establishing connections, improving overall performance.

Concurrency Settings

Optimizing concurrency settings ensures that multiple users can access the database simultaneously without performance degradation. Key parameters include:

Max Connections: Set an appropriate limit on the number of concurrent connections to prevent resource exhaustion.

Locking Mechanisms: Configure locking settings to minimize contention and deadlocks during concurrent operations. Consider using row-level locking instead of table-level locking for high-concurrency scenarios.

Disk I/O Optimization

Disk I/O performance is crucial for database efficiency. Consider the following strategies:

Storage Type: Use solid-state drives (SSDs) for faster read and write operations compared to traditional hard drives.

RAID Configuration: Implement RAID (Redundant Array of Independent Disks) configurations to improve redundancy and performance. RAID 10, for example, offers a good balance of speed and data protection.

File Organization: Optimize file organization by grouping related data together to minimize disk seeks during data retrieval.

Regular Maintenance

Regular maintenance is essential for sustaining optimal database performance over time. Scheduled maintenance tasks can help identify and address performance issues before they escalate.

Monitoring and Alerts

Implement monitoring solutions to continuously track database performance metrics. Set up alerts for critical thresholds, such as high CPU usage or slow query response times. Proactive monitoring allows DBAs to address issues promptly.

Performance Audits

Conduct regular performance audits to review database performance metrics, query execution plans, and indexing strategies. Identify bottlenecks and areas for improvement, and implement optimization strategies as needed.

Database Cleanup

Periodically perform database cleanup tasks to remove obsolete data, unused indexes, and unnecessary constraints. This helps reduce storage requirements and improve performance by streamlining operations.

Backup and Recovery Testing

Regularly test backup and recovery processes to ensure data integrity and availability. Performance during recovery operations can be crucial in disaster scenarios, and testing helps identify potential issues in advance.

Optimizing database performance is an ongoing process that involves a combination of query optimization, configuration tuning, and regular maintenance. By understanding key performance metrics, employing effective optimization strategies, and proactively monitoring performance, organizations can enhance the efficiency of their databases. A well-optimized database not only improves user experience but also contributes to overall system reliability and scalability. As data continues to grow and evolve, adopting a comprehensive approach to performance optimization is essential for success in today's data-driven landscape.

Chapter 7: Maintaining Database Security

Introduction to Database Security

Database security is a critical aspect of database management that focuses on protecting sensitive data from unauthorized access, breaches, and other malicious activities. As organizations increasingly rely on data-driven decision-making, ensuring the security of database systems is paramount. Effective database security encompasses a variety of practices, technologies, and policies designed to safeguard data integrity, confidentiality, and availability.

Importance of Database Security

The significance of database security cannot be overstated for several reasons:

Data Protection: Databases often store sensitive information, including personally identifiable information (PII), financial records, and intellectual property. Securing this data is essential to prevent unauthorized access and data breaches.

Regulatory Compliance: Many industries are subject to regulatory requirements governing data protection and privacy. Non-compliance can result in legal consequences and substantial fines. Implementing robust security measures helps organizations meet these obligations.

Reputation Management: A security breach can severely damage an organization's reputation. Protecting database systems helps maintain customer trust and confidence in the organization.

Operational Continuity: Security incidents can disrupt business operations, leading to downtime and financial losses. Ensuring database security contributes to overall business continuity and resilience.

Threats to Database Security

Understanding potential threats is vital for developing effective security measures. Common threats to database security include:

Unauthorized Access

Unauthorized access occurs when individuals gain access to database systems without proper permissions. This can happen due to weak authentication mechanisms, stolen credentials, or exploiting vulnerabilities.

SQL Injection Attacks

SQL injection attacks involve injecting malicious SQL code into queries to manipulate the database. This can result in data breaches, unauthorized data modification, or even complete database takeover. Attackers exploit vulnerabilities in web applications to execute arbitrary SQL commands.

Data Breaches

Data breaches occur when sensitive data is exposed to unauthorized individuals or entities. This can result from hacking, insider threats, or misconfigured security settings. Data breaches can have severe consequences, including financial losses and reputational damage.

Malware and Ransomware

Malware and ransomware can compromise database systems by encrypting data or exfiltrating sensitive information. Ransomware attacks often demand payment in exchange for restoring access to encrypted data, leading to significant operational disruptions.

Insider Threats

Insider threats involve malicious actions by employees or contractors with authorized access to the database. This can include data theft, sabotage, or unintentional data exposure. Organizations must address insider threats through effective access controls and monitoring.

Misconfiguration

Misconfigured database settings can create vulnerabilities that attackers can exploit. Common misconfigurations include weak passwords, excessive permissions, and inadequate logging practices. Regular security audits are essential to identify and remediate such issues.

Database Security Best Practices

Implementing robust security practices is essential for safeguarding database systems. Here are key strategies to enhance database security:

Access Control

Access control is a fundamental component of database security. It involves managing who can access the database and what actions they can perform. Key practices include:

Role-Based Access Control (RBAC): Implement RBAC to assign permissions based on user roles. This ensures that users have only the access necessary for their job functions, reducing the risk of unauthorized actions.

Least Privilege Principle: Grant users the minimum level of access required to perform their tasks. Regularly review and adjust permissions to prevent privilege creep.

Strong Authentication: Utilize strong authentication methods, such as multi-factor authentication (MFA), to enhance user verification. This adds an additional layer of security against unauthorized access.

Data Encryption

Data encryption protects sensitive information both at rest and in transit. Key considerations include:

Encryption at Rest: Use encryption to secure data stored in the database. This protects data from unauthorized access, especially in the event of a breach.
Encryption in Transit: Implement encryption protocols (e.g., SSL/TLS) to secure data transmitted between the database and applications. This prevents data interception during communication.

Regular Auditing and Monitoring

Regular auditing and monitoring of database activities are crucial for identifying potential security incidents. Key practices include:

Activity Logging: Enable logging of database activities, including user logins, data modifications, and access attempts. This creates a detailed record for forensic analysis and compliance reporting.
Real-Time Monitoring: Implement real-time monitoring solutions to detect suspicious activities or anomalies. Automated alerts can help identify potential threats before they escalate.

Database Hardening

Database hardening involves configuring the database to minimize vulnerabilities. Key practices include:

Remove Unused Features: Disable or remove unnecessary database features and services. This reduces the attack surface and minimizes potential entry points for attackers.

Patch Management: Regularly apply security patches and updates to the database management system (DBMS). Keeping the system up to date helps protect against known vulnerabilities.

Network Security: Restrict network access to the database using firewalls and Virtual Private Networks (VPNs). Ensure that only trusted IP addresses can connect to the database server.

Incident Response Planning

Having an incident response plan in place ensures a swift and effective response to security incidents. Key components of an incident response plan include:

Defined Roles and Responsibilities: Assign clear roles to team members for responding to security incidents. This ensures that everyone knows their responsibilities during a crisis.

Incident Detection and Reporting: Establish protocols for detecting and reporting security incidents. Early detection can help mitigate damage and facilitate timely response.

Post-Incident Review: Conduct a post-incident review to analyze the causes and impacts of the security incident. Use insights gained to improve security practices and prevent similar incidents in the future.

Regulatory Compliance

Organizations must adhere to various regulatory requirements governing data protection and privacy. Compliance with these regulations is essential for maintaining database security. Key regulations include:

General Data Protection Regulation (GDPR)

The GDPR imposes strict rules on the collection, processing, and storage of personal data for individuals within the European Union (EU). Key requirements include:

Data Protection by Design: Organizations must implement data protection measures from the outset of any project involving personal data.
User Consent: Obtain explicit consent from individuals before processing their personal data.
Data Breach Notification: Organizations must notify authorities and affected individuals within 72 hours of a data breach.

Health Insurance Portability and Accountability Act (HIPAA)

HIPAA sets standards for protecting sensitive patient information in the healthcare sector. Key requirements include:

Access Controls: Implement access controls to restrict unauthorized access to electronic protected health information (ePHI).
Data Encryption: Encrypt ePHI both in transit and at rest to protect patient information.
Audit Trails: Maintain audit trails to track access and modifications to ePHI.

Payment Card Industry Data Security Standard (PCI DSS)

The PCI DSS outlines security measures for organizations that handle credit card information. Key requirements include:

Secure Network: Implement firewalls and encryption to protect cardholder data.
Access Control Measures: Limit access to cardholder data on a need-to-know basis.
Regular Testing: Conduct regular vulnerability assessments and penetration testing to identify and address potential security weaknesses.

Maintaining database security is an ongoing and multifaceted process that requires a comprehensive approach. By understanding potential threats, implementing robust security practices, and adhering to regulatory compliance, organizations can protect sensitive data and ensure the integrity of their database systems. As the landscape of cybersecurity continues to evolve, remaining vigilant and proactive in database security is essential for safeguarding valuable organizational data and maintaining user trust.

Chapter 8: Data Backup and Recovery Strategies

Introduction to Data Backup and Recovery

Data backup and recovery are essential components of database management, ensuring that critical data is preserved and can be restored in the event of data loss, corruption, or disaster. A well-structured backup and recovery strategy not only protects against accidental deletions and hardware failures but also safeguards against malicious attacks such as ransomware. Organizations must prioritize these strategies to maintain data integrity and availability, thereby ensuring business continuity.

Importance of Data Backup and Recovery

The importance of effective backup and recovery strategies is underscored by several factors:

Data Loss Prevention: Data can be lost due to various reasons, including hardware malfunctions, software failures, human error, or natural disasters. A robust backup strategy mitigates the risks associated with data loss.

Business Continuity: In today's digital landscape, downtime can lead to significant financial losses and reputational damage.

A well-implemented recovery plan enables organizations to resume operations quickly after an incident.

Compliance Requirements: Many industries are subject to regulations that mandate data retention and recovery capabilities. Adhering to these regulations is crucial to avoid penalties and maintain customer trust.

Protection Against Cyber Threats: With the rise of cyberattacks, including ransomware, maintaining regular backups provides a safety net. Organizations can recover their data without succumbing to ransom demands.

Types of Backup

Understanding the various types of backups is crucial for designing an effective backup strategy. Each type serves a specific purpose and can be utilized based on organizational needs.

Full Backup

A full backup involves creating a complete copy of the entire database. This type of backup is comprehensive but can be time-consuming and resource-intensive. Key characteristics include:

Complete Data Copy: A full backup captures all data, including tables, indexes, and configurations, ensuring that a complete restore point is available.

Restoration Simplicity: Restoring from a full backup is straightforward, as it requires only one backup set.

Resource Intensive: Full backups consume significant storage space and require substantial time to complete, making them less practical for frequent backups.

Incremental Backup

Incremental backups capture only the changes made since the last backup, whether it was a full or incremental backup. This approach is more efficient in terms of time and storage. Key aspects include:

Space Efficiency: Incremental backups require less storage space than full backups, as they only store the changed data.

Faster Backups: Since only the modified data is backed up, incremental backups can be completed quickly, allowing for more frequent backup schedules.

Restoration Complexity: Restoring from an incremental backup can be more complex, as it requires the last full backup and all subsequent incremental backups.

Differential Backup

Differential backups capture all changes made since the last full backup. This type strikes a balance between full and incremental backups. Key features include:

Moderate Storage Requirement: Differential backups require more storage than incremental backups but less than full backups since they capture all changes since the last full backup.
Simpler Restoration Process: Restoration is simpler than with incremental backups, as it only requires the last full backup and the most recent differential backup.
Longer Backup Times: As time progresses since the last full backup, differential backups can take longer to complete as they capture more changes.

Mirror Backup

A mirror backup creates an exact copy of the database at a specific point in time. This method is primarily used for redundancy rather than long-term retention. Key points include:

Real-Time Reflection: Mirror backups provide real-time data protection, as they replicate changes almost immediately.
No Historical Versioning: Unlike other backups, mirror backups do not keep historical versions of the data, making them unsuitable for scenarios where versioning is essential.
Storage Requirements: Since mirror backups are complete copies, they require substantial storage resources.

Backup Strategies

Implementing a robust backup strategy involves considering factors such as data criticality, recovery time objectives (RTO), and recovery point objectives (RPO). Here are essential strategies to guide the backup process:

Backup Frequency

Determining the frequency of backups is crucial for minimizing data loss. Consider the following guidelines:

Critical Data: For critical data that changes frequently, consider daily or even hourly backups to ensure minimal data loss in case of an incident.

Less Critical Data: For less critical data, weekly or bi-weekly backups may be sufficient. Tailor the frequency to match the importance and volatility of the data.

Backup Rotation

Employing a backup rotation scheme ensures that multiple backup sets are available for recovery. Common rotation methods include:

Grandfather-Father-Son (GFS): This method involves maintaining a set of daily, weekly, and monthly backups. For example, daily backups are kept for a week (sons), weekly backups are kept for a month (fathers), and monthly backups are stored for a year (grandfathers).

7-14-30 Scheme: Under this approach, backups are retained for specific timeframes (e.g., daily for 7 days, weekly for 14 weeks, and monthly for 30 months).

Offsite Storage

Storing backups offsite is essential for disaster recovery. This protects backups from local disasters such as fires, floods, or theft. Key considerations include:

Cloud Storage: Utilize cloud storage solutions to maintain offsite backups. Cloud providers offer redundancy and geographic distribution, enhancing data protection.
Physical Offsite: For organizations with strict data security requirements, consider using physical media (e.g., external hard drives) stored in secure offsite locations.

Testing Backup and Recovery Procedures

Regular testing of backup and recovery procedures is critical to ensure their effectiveness. Key steps include:

Scheduled Recovery Drills: Conduct regular drills to simulate data recovery scenarios. This ensures that team members are familiar with the recovery process and can identify potential issues.
Validation of Backup Integrity: Periodically validate backup files to ensure they are not corrupted and can be restored successfully. Regular checks prevent surprises during recovery efforts.

Recovery Strategies

A well-defined recovery strategy is essential for ensuring that data can be restored promptly after an incident. Key components of an effective recovery strategy include:

Defining Recovery Objectives

Establish clear recovery objectives to guide the recovery process:

Recovery Time Objective (RTO): The RTO defines the maximum acceptable downtime after a data loss event. It informs how quickly the database must be restored to minimize disruption.
Recovery Point Objective (RPO): The RPO indicates the maximum acceptable amount of data loss measured in time. It guides backup frequency to ensure data is preserved within acceptable limits.

Restoration Procedures

Clearly document the restoration procedures for different scenarios. Key elements include:

Step-by-Step Instructions: Provide detailed instructions for restoring from various backup types (full, incremental, differential). This documentation should be readily accessible to the recovery team.
Roles and Responsibilities: Assign specific roles to team members for the recovery process. Clearly defined

responsibilities ensure an organized response during critical incidents.

Disaster Recovery Plan

Integrate backup and recovery strategies into a broader disaster recovery plan (DRP). Key considerations include:

Risk Assessment: Identify potential risks that could impact data availability and develop strategies to mitigate those risks.
Communication Protocols: Establish communication protocols to inform stakeholders during and after a data loss event. Clear communication is essential for maintaining transparency and managing expectations.
Regular Review and Updates: Periodically review and update the disaster recovery plan to reflect changes in infrastructure, business processes, or data requirements.

Data backup and recovery strategies are essential for safeguarding critical information and ensuring business continuity in the face of data loss events. By understanding the various types of backups, implementing robust backup strategies, and developing comprehensive recovery plans, organizations can protect themselves against potential threats and minimize the impact of data loss. As data continues to grow and the threat landscape evolves, organizations must remain vigilant and proactive in their backup and recovery efforts to safeguard their valuable information assets.

Chapter 9: Data Migration Techniques

Introduction to Data Migration

Data migration is the process of transferring data from one system, storage, or format to another. It is a critical task for organizations undergoing system upgrades, transitioning to cloud services, consolidating data sources, or implementing new applications. Effective data migration ensures that data integrity is maintained while minimizing downtime and disruptions to business operations. Given the increasing volume and complexity of data in modern enterprises, understanding the techniques and best practices for successful data migration is essential.

Importance of Data Migration

The significance of data migration can be attributed to several factors:

System Upgrades: Organizations frequently upgrade their systems or applications to leverage new functionalities, improve performance, or enhance security. Data migration is essential to ensure that legacy data is seamlessly transferred to the new environment.

Cloud Adoption: As organizations increasingly adopt cloud services, migrating data to the cloud becomes necessary. This transition allows for greater scalability, flexibility, and cost-efficiency.

Data Consolidation: Mergers and acquisitions often result in the need to consolidate disparate data sources into a unified system. Effective data migration enables organizations to achieve a single source of truth.

Regulatory Compliance: Certain regulations require organizations to maintain specific data management practices, which may necessitate data migration to comply with updated standards.

Types of Data Migration

Understanding the various types of data migration is crucial for selecting the appropriate approach for specific projects. The following are common types of data migration:

Storage Migration

Storage migration involves transferring data from one storage system to another. This may include moving data from on-premises storage to cloud storage or from older storage hardware to newer, more efficient systems. Key aspects include:

Optimization: Organizations may migrate data to optimize storage costs or improve access speeds.

Cloud Integration: As businesses adopt cloud solutions, storage migration enables the seamless transfer of data to cloud environments.

Database Migration

Database migration involves moving data between different database management systems (DBMS) or upgrading to a new version of the same DBMS. Key considerations include:

Schema Compatibility: Ensuring that the schema of the new database is compatible with the data being migrated is crucial to avoid data corruption.

Data Transformation: Database migration may require transforming data formats or structures to align with the new DBMS requirements.

Application Migration

Application migration involves moving data associated with specific applications, often necessitating adjustments to both the data and the application itself. This type can include:

Legacy Application Modernization: Organizations may migrate data from outdated applications to new platforms that offer improved functionality and performance.

Integration with New Systems: When implementing new applications, data must be migrated to ensure continuity and functionality.

Cloud Migration

Cloud migration refers to moving data, applications, or workloads to cloud environments. Organizations may migrate to public, private, or hybrid cloud setups. Key factors include:

Scalability: Cloud migration allows organizations to scale their data storage and processing capabilities according to demand.
Cost Efficiency: Transitioning to cloud services can reduce infrastructure costs, allowing for better resource allocation.

Data Migration Techniques

When planning a data migration project, organizations must choose appropriate migration techniques based on their specific needs. Below are key techniques to consider:

Big Bang Migration

Big Bang migration involves transferring all data at once during a scheduled downtime. This technique can be efficient but carries certain risks and considerations:

Pros:
Quick implementation, as all data is moved in one go.
Easier to manage, as the entire process occurs within a defined timeframe.
Cons:

Requires significant downtime, which can disrupt business operations.
Higher risk of data loss or corruption if issues arise during the transfer.

Big Bang migrations are suitable for smaller datasets or less critical systems where downtime can be accommodated.

Trickle Migration

Trickle migration, also known as phased migration, involves transferring data incrementally over time. This technique allows organizations to minimize downtime and maintain continuous operations. Key characteristics include:

Pros:
Reduces downtime, as data can be migrated in phases without disrupting business processes.
Lower risk of data loss, as the migration is spread out and can be monitored more closely.
Cons:
Can be more complex to manage, as multiple migrations may be ongoing simultaneously.
Longer overall migration timeline.

Trickle migration is ideal for large datasets, critical systems, or scenarios where business continuity is a top priority.

Hybrid Migration

Hybrid migration combines elements of both Big Bang and trickle migrations. Organizations may use this approach to balance the benefits of both techniques based on specific requirements. Key considerations include:

Selective Data Migration: Critical data may be migrated using the Big Bang approach while less critical data is moved gradually.
Custom Scheduling: Different parts of the data can be migrated according to their urgency or importance, allowing for flexibility in planning.

Hybrid migration is beneficial for organizations that need to manage complex environments or specific application requirements.

Data Migration Process

Executing a successful data migration involves several key steps. Each stage must be meticulously planned and executed to ensure a smooth transition.

Assessment and Planning

The first step in the data migration process involves assessing the existing data environment and creating a comprehensive migration plan. Key activities include:

Data Inventory: Conduct a thorough inventory of the data to be migrated. Understand its structure, format, volume, and relevance.

Define Objectives: Establish clear objectives for the migration project, including desired outcomes, timelines, and resource requirements.

Risk Analysis: Identify potential risks and challenges associated with the migration, such as data loss, downtime, or compatibility issues. Develop mitigation strategies.

Data Mapping and Transformation

Once the planning is complete, the next step involves mapping the source data to the target system and preparing it for migration. Key considerations include:

Schema Mapping: Map the data structure from the source system to the target system. This includes identifying how tables, fields, and relationships will be transferred.

Data Transformation: If necessary, transform data formats to align with the target system's requirements. This may include converting data types, cleaning data, or enriching data with additional information.

Migration Execution

The migration execution phase involves the actual transfer of data. This phase can vary significantly based on the chosen migration technique. Key activities include:

Initial Transfer: For Big Bang migrations, perform the full data transfer during a scheduled downtime. For trickle migrations, begin transferring data in phases according to the defined schedule.

Monitoring: Continuously monitor the migration process to identify any issues or errors. Implement automated alerts to notify the team of potential problems.

Validation and Testing

After the migration is complete, it is essential to validate the migrated data to ensure accuracy and integrity. Key steps include:

Data Comparison: Compare the source data with the migrated data to ensure consistency. Check for missing records, data corruption, or discrepancies.

Testing Functionality: Test the target system to verify that applications and processes function as expected with the migrated data.

Post-Migration Review

The final step involves conducting a post-migration review to assess the success of the migration project and identify areas for improvement. Key activities include:

Documentation: Document the entire migration process, including challenges encountered, solutions implemented, and lessons learned.

Feedback and Improvements: Gather feedback from stakeholders and team members involved in the migration. Use this information to refine future migration strategies and processes.

Challenges in Data Migration

While data migration is a crucial process, organizations may encounter several challenges during execution. Being aware of these challenges can help in proactive planning and risk mitigation.

Data Quality Issues

Data quality is a common challenge in migration projects. Inaccurate, inconsistent, or incomplete data can lead to significant problems during and after migration. Key strategies include:

Data Cleansing: Implement data cleansing processes before migration to identify and rectify data quality issues.

Validation Rules: Establish validation rules to ensure that only high-quality data is migrated.

Downtime and Business Disruption

Minimizing downtime during migration is crucial for maintaining business operations. Challenges include:

Planning for Downtime: Organizations must carefully plan migration schedules to minimize disruption during peak business hours.
Communication: Clearly communicate with stakeholders regarding potential downtime and expected outcomes to manage expectations.

Complexity of Legacy Systems

Legacy systems may present compatibility and integration challenges during migration. Key strategies include:

Assess Compatibility: Evaluate the compatibility of legacy systems with the target environment to identify potential issues.
Gradual Migration: For complex legacy systems, consider gradual migration approaches to reduce risks and manage challenges effectively.

Resource Constraints

Data migration projects often require significant resources, including time, budget, and personnel. Challenges include:

Resource Allocation: Ensure that adequate resources are allocated to the migration project to avoid delays and overruns.

Team Training: Invest in training for team members involved in the migration to ensure they are equipped with the necessary skills and knowledge.

Data migration is a vital process for organizations looking to modernize their data management practices, adopt new technologies, or consolidate systems. By understanding the various types of data migration, employing appropriate techniques, and following a structured process, organizations can successfully migrate their data while minimizing risks and disruptions. As data continues to grow and evolve, effective data migration strategies will be essential for maintaining data integrity, enhancing business operations, and ensuring compliance with regulatory requirements.

Chapter 10: Data Governance Framework

Introduction to Data Governance

Data governance refers to the comprehensive management of data availability, usability, integrity, and security within an organization. A robust data governance framework ensures that data is effectively managed and utilized, promoting accountability, compliance, and strategic decision-making. As organizations become increasingly data-driven, establishing clear governance policies and processes is essential to harness the full value of their data assets.

Importance of Data Governance

The significance of data governance is underscored by several factors:

Data Quality Improvement: Effective governance ensures data quality by establishing standards and practices for data collection, storage, and usage. High-quality data enhances decision-making and operational efficiency.

Regulatory Compliance: Many industries face strict regulatory requirements concerning data privacy and protection. A solid governance framework helps organizations comply with laws and regulations, reducing the risk of penalties.

Data Security and Privacy: Governance frameworks define roles and responsibilities for data access and protection, minimizing the risk of data breaches and ensuring that sensitive information is safeguarded.

Enhanced Decision-Making: By ensuring that data is accurate and accessible, organizations can make informed decisions based on reliable insights, driving better business outcomes.

Key Components of Data Governance

A comprehensive data governance framework comprises several key components that work together to create an effective governance structure.

Data Stewardship

Data stewardship involves assigning responsibility for managing data assets within the organization. Key aspects include:

Roles and Responsibilities: Define clear roles for data stewards, data owners, and data custodians, ensuring accountability for data quality and compliance.

Cross-Functional Collaboration: Encourage collaboration among different departments, as effective data governance requires input and commitment from various stakeholders.

Data Policies and Standards

Establishing data policies and standards is essential for guiding data management practices. Key considerations include:

Data Classification: Develop a classification system for data based on sensitivity, usage, and regulatory requirements. This helps in determining appropriate access controls and handling procedures.

Data Quality Standards: Define quality metrics and standards for data collection, validation, and maintenance, ensuring that data meets organizational expectations.

Data Architecture and Management

A well-defined data architecture provides the structure necessary for managing data effectively. Key elements include:

Data Models: Create data models that outline how data is organized, stored, and accessed. This ensures consistency and clarity in data management practices.

Metadata Management: Implement metadata management practices to provide context and meaning to data assets, improving data discoverability and usability.

Compliance and Risk Management

Ensuring compliance with regulations and managing risks associated with data is critical. Key strategies include:

Regulatory Alignment: Stay informed about relevant laws and regulations affecting data management and ensure that governance practices align with these requirements.

Risk Assessment: Regularly conduct risk assessments to identify potential threats to data security and integrity, and develop strategies to mitigate these risks.

Data Access and Security

Establishing protocols for data access and security is essential for protecting sensitive information. Key practices include:

Access Controls: Implement role-based access controls to limit data access based on user roles and responsibilities, ensuring that only authorized individuals can access sensitive data.

Data Encryption: Utilize encryption to protect data both at rest and in transit, safeguarding it from unauthorized access.

Data Governance Framework Models

Organizations can adopt various models for their data governance frameworks, depending on their specific needs and structures. Here are some common models:

Centralized Governance Model

In a centralized governance model, a dedicated team oversees all data governance activities across the organization. Key characteristics include:

Single Point of Accountability: A centralized team is responsible for data policies, standards, and compliance, ensuring consistency across the organization.

Streamlined Decision-Making: With a clear hierarchy, decision-making related to data governance can be more efficient, allowing for quicker responses to emerging issues.

Decentralized Governance Model

In a decentralized governance model, individual departments or business units manage their data governance practices. Key features include:

Flexibility: Each department can tailor its governance practices to meet specific needs and requirements, allowing for greater adaptability.

Empowerment: Departments take ownership of their data, fostering a culture of accountability and responsibility.

Hybrid Governance Model

The hybrid governance model combines elements of both centralized and decentralized approaches. Key aspects include:

Shared Responsibility: While a central governance team establishes overarching policies and standards, individual departments retain the authority to implement practices that suit their specific contexts.

Collaboration: Encourages collaboration between the central team and departmental stakeholders, balancing consistency with flexibility.

Implementing a Data Governance Framework

Establishing a data governance framework requires a structured approach. Organizations should follow these steps to ensure successful implementation:

Define Objectives and Scope

Before implementation, organizations must define the objectives of their data governance initiative. Key activities include:

Identifying Goals: Determine the primary goals of data governance, such as improving data quality, ensuring compliance, or enhancing data security.
Scoping the Initiative: Define the scope of the data governance framework, including the types of data, systems, and processes that will be governed.

Engage Stakeholders

Engaging stakeholders across the organization is crucial for building support and ensuring successful implementation. Key considerations include:

Identifying Key Stakeholders: Identify key stakeholders, including data owners, data stewards, and executive sponsors, to ensure representation from various departments.

Building a Governance Committee: Establish a cross-functional governance committee responsible for guiding the implementation of the framework and addressing challenges.

Develop Policies and Standards

Once stakeholders are engaged, organizations should develop clear policies and standards to guide data management practices. Key steps include:

Drafting Policies: Collaborate with stakeholders to draft data governance policies that address data quality, security, access, and compliance.

Defining Standards: Establish data quality standards, classification schemes, and metadata management practices to provide guidance for data management.

Implement Processes and Tools

Implementing processes and tools is essential for operationalizing the data governance framework. Key considerations include:

Selecting Tools: Choose appropriate data governance tools that facilitate data management, quality monitoring, and compliance tracking.

Establishing Processes: Define processes for data collection, validation, access control, and reporting to ensure that policies and standards are effectively applied.

Monitor and Review

Ongoing monitoring and review are crucial for ensuring the effectiveness of the data governance framework. Key activities include:

Performance Metrics: Establish key performance indicators (KPIs) to measure the effectiveness of governance practices and data quality.
Regular Reviews: Conduct regular reviews of governance policies and processes to identify areas for improvement and adapt to changing organizational needs.

Challenges in Data Governance

While establishing a data governance framework offers significant benefits, organizations may encounter challenges during implementation. Being aware of these challenges can help organizations proactively address them.

Cultural Resistance

Cultural resistance to change can impede the implementation of data governance initiatives. Key strategies to overcome this challenge include:

Change Management: Implement change management practices to facilitate a smooth transition to new governance processes.

Awareness Campaigns: Educate employees about the importance of data governance and how it contributes to organizational success.

Lack of Resources

Data governance initiatives may require significant resources, including personnel, tools, and budget. Key considerations include:

Resource Allocation: Ensure that adequate resources are allocated to the governance initiative to support implementation and ongoing management.

Building a Business Case: Develop a compelling business case to secure funding and support for data governance initiatives.

Complex Data Environments

As organizations accumulate vast amounts of data from various sources, managing this complexity can be challenging. Key strategies include:

Data Inventory: Conduct a comprehensive data inventory to understand the data landscape and identify areas for governance.

Modular Approaches: Implement modular governance approaches that allow organizations to address specific data challenges incrementally.

Evolving Regulations

Data governance must adapt to changing regulatory requirements, which can be challenging for organizations. Key strategies include:

Regulatory Monitoring: Stay informed about relevant regulations and ensure that governance practices align with legal requirements.

Agility in Governance: Design the governance framework to be flexible and adaptable, allowing for quick adjustments in response to regulatory changes.

Establishing a robust data governance framework is essential for organizations seeking to maximize the value of their data assets while ensuring compliance, security, and quality. By understanding the key components of data governance, adopting suitable governance models, and following a structured implementation process, organizations can create a strong foundation for effective data management. As the data landscape continues to evolve, a well-defined governance framework will empower organizations to navigate challenges, make informed decisions, and drive business success through data-driven insights.

Chapter 11: Data Security Measures

Introduction to Data Security

Data security encompasses the practices, processes, and technologies designed to protect data from unauthorized access, corruption, theft, or loss. With the increasing amount of sensitive information stored and processed by organizations, implementing robust data security measures is critical to safeguarding data assets. Effective data security not only protects against cyber threats but also ensures compliance with regulatory requirements and maintains customer trust.

Importance of Data Security

The importance of data security can be attributed to several key factors:

Protection of Sensitive Information: Organizations handle various types of sensitive data, including personal identifiable information (PII), financial records, and intellectual property. Effective security measures are essential to protect this data from breaches.

Compliance with Regulations: Many industries are subject to regulations that mandate stringent data security practices. Non-compliance can result in severe penalties and legal consequences.

Mitigation of Cyber Threats: Cyberattacks are increasingly sophisticated, targeting organizations of all sizes. A robust data security strategy helps mitigate the risks associated with these threats.

Preservation of Reputation: Data breaches can significantly damage an organization's reputation. Implementing strong security measures helps maintain customer trust and brand integrity.

Key Data Security Concepts

Understanding key data security concepts is crucial for developing an effective security strategy. Here are some foundational elements:

Confidentiality

Confidentiality ensures that sensitive information is accessible only to authorized individuals. Key practices to maintain confidentiality include:

Access Controls: Implementing role-based access controls (RBAC) to restrict data access based on user roles and responsibilities.

Data Encryption: Encrypting sensitive data both at rest and in transit to protect it from unauthorized access.

Integrity

Data integrity ensures that information remains accurate, consistent, and unaltered throughout its lifecycle. Key practices include:

Data Validation: Implementing validation checks to ensure that data entered into systems meets predefined criteria.
Change Monitoring: Utilizing audit trails to track changes made to data, enabling organizations to detect and address unauthorized alterations.

Availability

Availability ensures that data is accessible to authorized users when needed. Key practices include:

Redundancy: Implementing redundant systems and backups to ensure data availability in the event of hardware failures or disasters.
Disaster Recovery Plans: Developing comprehensive disaster recovery plans to restore access to data in the event of a significant incident.

Data Security Measures

Organizations can implement various data security measures to protect their data assets. Below are essential security practices to consider:

Data Classification

Data classification involves categorizing data based on its sensitivity and importance. Key steps include:

Identifying Data Types: Identify and categorize data types (e.g., public, internal, confidential, sensitive) to determine the appropriate security measures.

Establishing Handling Procedures: Define handling procedures for each data classification level, including access controls and sharing protocols.

Access Control Mechanisms

Implementing robust access control mechanisms is essential for protecting sensitive data. Key strategies include:

Role-Based Access Control (RBAC): Assign permissions based on user roles, ensuring that individuals only have access to the data necessary for their job functions.

Multi-Factor Authentication (MFA): Implement MFA to enhance security by requiring multiple forms of verification before granting access.

Data Encryption

Data encryption is a crucial practice for safeguarding sensitive information. Key considerations include:

Encryption at Rest: Encrypting data stored on servers, databases, or storage devices to protect it from unauthorized access.

Encryption in Transit: Using secure protocols (e.g., HTTPS, SSL/TLS) to encrypt data during transmission, preventing interception by malicious actors.

Network Security

Network security measures protect data as it moves across networks. Key strategies include:

Firewalls: Deploying firewalls to monitor and control incoming and outgoing network traffic based on predetermined security rules.

Intrusion Detection and Prevention Systems (IDPS): Implementing IDPS to detect and respond to potential security breaches in real-time.

Regular Security Audits and Assessments

Conducting regular security audits and assessments is essential for identifying vulnerabilities and ensuring compliance. Key practices include:

Vulnerability Scanning: Performing regular vulnerability scans to identify potential security weaknesses in systems and applications.

Penetration Testing: Conducting penetration tests to simulate cyberattacks and assess the effectiveness of security measures.

Data Backup and Recovery

Implementing robust data backup and recovery strategies is crucial for ensuring data availability. Key strategies include:

Regular Backups: Scheduling regular backups of critical data to protect against data loss due to hardware failures or cyber incidents.

Disaster Recovery Planning: Developing and testing disaster recovery plans to ensure swift data restoration in the event of a significant incident.

Compliance and Regulatory Requirements

Organizations must adhere to various compliance and regulatory requirements related to data security. Key regulations include:

General Data Protection Regulation (GDPR)

The GDPR is a comprehensive data protection regulation that governs the processing of personal data within the European Union. Key requirements include:

Consent: Organizations must obtain explicit consent from individuals before processing their personal data.

Data Breach Notifications: Organizations must report data breaches to relevant authorities within 72 hours of discovery.

Health Insurance Portability and Accountability Act (HIPAA)

HIPAA establishes data security and privacy requirements for healthcare organizations in the United States. Key provisions include:

Protected Health Information (PHI): Organizations must implement safeguards to protect PHI from unauthorized access and disclosure.
Security Rule: The Security Rule outlines standards for the protection of electronic PHI, including administrative, physical, and technical safeguards.

Payment Card Industry Data Security Standard (PCI DSS)

PCI DSS sets security standards for organizations that handle credit card information. Key requirements include:

Data Protection: Organizations must protect cardholder data through encryption, access controls, and regular security testing.
Monitoring and Testing: Organizations must monitor networks and conduct regular security testing to identify vulnerabilities.

Challenges in Data Security

While implementing data security measures is essential, organizations may face several challenges in doing so. Key challenges include:

Evolving Cyber Threats

Cyber threats are constantly evolving, requiring organizations to stay vigilant and adapt their security measures. Key strategies include:

Continuous Monitoring: Implement continuous monitoring practices to detect and respond to emerging threats in real-time.
Threat Intelligence: Utilize threat intelligence to stay informed about current attack trends and vulnerabilities.

Employee Awareness and Training

Employees play a crucial role in data security, and lack of awareness can lead to vulnerabilities. Key practices include:

Security Training: Provide regular security training to employees to raise awareness of data security best practices and potential threats.
Phishing Simulations: Conduct phishing simulations to test employee responses to potential social engineering attacks.

Complexity of Data Environments

The complexity of modern data environments, including cloud services and hybrid infrastructures, can complicate security efforts. Key considerations include:

Unified Security Strategy: Develop a unified security strategy that encompasses on-premises and cloud environments to ensure comprehensive protection.

Integration of Security Tools: Ensure that security tools can integrate seamlessly across different systems and platforms to provide holistic protection.

Balancing Security and Usability

Organizations must balance the need for strong security measures with user experience. Key strategies include:

User-Centric Security: Design security measures that prioritize user experience while still providing robust protection.

Feedback Mechanisms: Implement feedback mechanisms to gather input from users on security measures, allowing for continuous improvement.

Data security is a critical aspect of modern data management, essential for protecting sensitive information and maintaining compliance with regulations. By understanding key security concepts, implementing robust security measures, and addressing the challenges associated with data security, organizations can safeguard their data assets and mitigate risks. As the threat landscape continues to evolve, maintaining a proactive and adaptable approach to data security will be crucial for ensuring the confidentiality, integrity, and availability of data.

Chapter 12: Data Compliance and Regulatory Frameworks

Introduction to Data Compliance

Data compliance refers to the process of ensuring that an organization's data management practices adhere to legal, regulatory, and industry standards. With the increasing importance of data privacy and protection, organizations must navigate a complex landscape of regulations that govern how data is collected, stored, processed, and shared. Understanding and implementing data compliance frameworks is essential for mitigating legal risks, enhancing data security, and maintaining customer trust.

Importance of Data Compliance

The significance of data compliance can be highlighted through several key points:

Legal Obligation: Organizations are legally required to comply with various data protection regulations. Failure to do so can result in severe penalties, including fines and legal actions.

Trust and Reputation: Compliance with data protection laws fosters trust among customers and stakeholders. Organizations that prioritize data compliance are often viewed more favorably.

Risk Mitigation: Effective compliance programs help organizations identify and mitigate risks associated with data breaches, thus reducing potential liabilities.

Operational Efficiency: Implementing data compliance measures can lead to improved data management practices, enhancing overall operational efficiency.

Key Data Compliance Regulations

Organizations must be aware of several key regulations that govern data protection and privacy. Below are some of the most influential data compliance regulations:

General Data Protection Regulation (GDPR)

The GDPR is a comprehensive regulation enacted by the European Union that governs the processing of personal data of EU residents. Key provisions include:

Data Subject Rights: The GDPR grants individuals various rights regarding their data, including the right to access, rectify, and erase personal information.

Consent Requirements: Organizations must obtain explicit consent from individuals before collecting or processing their personal data.

Data Breach Notifications: In the event of a data breach, organizations are required to notify affected individuals and relevant authorities within 72 hours.

Health Insurance Portability and Accountability Act (HIPAA)

HIPAA establishes standards for the protection of sensitive patient information in the United States. Key provisions include:

Protected Health Information (PHI): HIPAA defines PHI and mandates safeguards to protect it from unauthorized access and disclosure.
Security Rule: The Security Rule outlines requirements for the confidentiality, integrity, and availability of electronic PHI, including administrative, physical, and technical safeguards.

California Consumer Privacy Act (CCPA)

The CCPA provides California residents with enhanced rights regarding their personal information. Key provisions include:

Consumer Rights: California residents have the right to know what personal data is being collected, to whom it is sold, and to request deletion of their data.
Opt-Out Option: Organizations must provide consumers with the option to opt-out of the sale of their personal information.

Payment Card Industry Data Security Standard (PCI DSS)

PCI DSS sets security standards for organizations that handle credit card information. Key requirements include:

Data Protection: Organizations must protect cardholder data through encryption, access controls, and regular security testing.
Monitoring and Testing: Organizations must implement monitoring mechanisms to track access to cardholder data and conduct regular vulnerability assessments.

Developing a Data Compliance Framework

To effectively navigate the landscape of data compliance, organizations should develop a comprehensive compliance framework. Key steps in this process include:

Conduct a Compliance Assessment

The first step in developing a compliance framework is conducting a thorough assessment of existing data practices. Key activities include:

Data Inventory: Identify and categorize all data assets within the organization to understand what data is being collected, processed, and stored.
Regulatory Mapping: Map applicable regulations to the organization's data practices to identify compliance gaps and areas of risk.

Establish Data Governance Policies

Establishing clear data governance policies is essential for guiding compliance efforts. Key considerations include:

Data Classification: Define data classification schemes to categorize data based on its sensitivity and regulatory requirements.
Access Controls: Implement access control policies to restrict data access based on user roles and responsibilities.

Implement Technical Controls

Technical controls are essential for protecting data and ensuring compliance with regulatory requirements. Key measures include:

Encryption: Encrypt sensitive data at rest and in transit to protect it from unauthorized access.
Monitoring and Auditing: Implement monitoring tools to track data access and usage, enabling organizations to detect potential breaches and ensure compliance.

Train Employees on Compliance Practices

Employee awareness and training are crucial for fostering a culture of compliance within the organization. Key activities include:

Training Programs: Develop and implement training programs that educate employees about data protection regulations and their responsibilities.

Regular Updates: Provide regular updates on changes to data protection laws and organizational policies to keep employees informed.

Conduct Regular Compliance Audits

Regular audits are essential for assessing the effectiveness of compliance measures and identifying areas for improvement. Key practices include:

Internal Audits: Conduct regular internal audits to evaluate compliance with established policies and regulatory requirements.

Third-Party Assessments: Consider engaging external auditors to provide an independent assessment of the organization's compliance efforts.

Data Compliance Challenges

While organizations strive to achieve data compliance, they may encounter several challenges. Understanding these challenges can help organizations develop effective strategies to address them.

Evolving Regulations

Data protection regulations are continually evolving, requiring organizations to stay informed and adapt their compliance practices accordingly. Key strategies include:

Regulatory Monitoring: Establish mechanisms for monitoring changes to data protection laws and regulations that may impact compliance efforts.

Agility in Compliance: Design compliance processes to be flexible and adaptable, allowing for quick adjustments in response to regulatory changes.

Complex Data Environments

The complexity of modern data environments, including cloud services and hybrid infrastructures, can complicate compliance efforts. Key considerations include:

Unified Compliance Strategy: Develop a unified compliance strategy that encompasses on-premises and cloud data, ensuring comprehensive adherence to regulations.

Integration of Compliance Tools: Implement compliance tools that can integrate across different systems and platforms to streamline compliance management.

Resource Constraints

Achieving and maintaining data compliance often requires significant resources, including time, personnel, and budget. Key practices include:

Resource Allocation: Ensure that adequate resources are allocated to compliance initiatives to support implementation and ongoing management.

Building a Business Case: Develop a compelling business case to secure funding and support for data compliance programs.

Cultural Resistance

Cultural resistance to change can impede compliance efforts, especially in organizations with established practices. Key strategies include:

Change Management: Implement change management practices to facilitate a smooth transition to new compliance processes.

Leadership Support: Secure support from leadership to promote a culture of compliance and accountability throughout the organization.

Data compliance is a critical aspect of modern data management, essential for protecting sensitive information and ensuring adherence to legal and regulatory requirements. By understanding key regulations, developing a comprehensive compliance framework, and addressing the challenges associated with compliance, organizations can effectively navigate the complexities of data protection. As the regulatory landscape continues to evolve, maintaining a proactive and adaptable approach to data compliance will be crucial for safeguarding data assets and building trust with customers and stakeholders.

Chapter 13: Data Integration Strategies

Introduction to Data Integration

Data integration is the process of combining data from different sources into a unified view, enabling organizations to analyze and utilize data effectively. In today's data-driven environment, where organizations rely on diverse data sources—ranging from databases and applications to cloud services—implementing effective data integration strategies is crucial for informed decision-making, operational efficiency, and maintaining a competitive edge.

Importance of Data Integration

The significance of data integration can be highlighted through several key points:

Comprehensive Insights: By integrating data from multiple sources, organizations gain a holistic view of their operations, customers, and market trends, facilitating better decision-making.

Improved Data Quality: Data integration processes often include cleansing and standardization steps, enhancing the overall quality and consistency of data.

Enhanced Efficiency: Automated data integration reduces manual data handling, minimizing errors and saving time, which improves overall operational efficiency.

Real-Time Analytics: Effective integration allows for real-time data access, enabling organizations to respond quickly to changing conditions and opportunities.

Types of Data Integration

Organizations can adopt various types of data integration methods, each suited to specific use cases and needs. Here are the primary types:

Batch Data Integration

Batch data integration involves collecting and processing data at scheduled intervals rather than in real time. Key characteristics include:

Scheduled Processing: Data is aggregated and processed periodically (e.g., hourly, daily, weekly), making it suitable for environments where real-time data is not critical.

Data Warehousing: Often used in data warehousing scenarios, where large volumes of historical data are combined for analysis.

Real-Time Data Integration

Real-time data integration enables the immediate processing and synchronization of data across systems as it is generated. Key features include:

Continuous Data Flow: Data is continuously integrated, allowing organizations to respond to changes instantly.
Event-Driven Architecture: Often implemented using event-driven architectures, such as message queues and streaming technologies.

Federated Data Integration

Federated data integration provides a virtual view of data from multiple sources without physically moving or transforming the data. Key aspects include:

Data Virtualization: Users can query data across disparate sources as if it were a single database, facilitating access without data duplication.
Minimal Data Movement: Reduces the need for data replication and storage, which can lower costs and enhance data governance.

Cloud Data Integration

As organizations increasingly adopt cloud solutions, cloud data integration has become vital. Key considerations include:

Cloud-to-Cloud Integration: Connecting different cloud services (e.g., SaaS applications) to ensure seamless data flow.
Hybrid Integration: Combining on-premises and cloud data sources, allowing organizations to leverage existing systems while adopting cloud technologies.

Data Integration Approaches

Organizations can adopt various approaches to implement data integration effectively. The choice of approach depends on factors such as data complexity, volume, and specific business needs.

ETL (Extract, Transform, Load)

ETL is a traditional data integration approach that involves extracting data from source systems, transforming it into a suitable format, and loading it into a target system, such as a data warehouse. Key steps include:

Extraction: Collecting data from various sources, including databases, applications, and flat files.
Transformation: Cleaning, validating, and transforming data to ensure it meets quality standards and is structured appropriately for analysis.
Loading: Inserting the transformed data into the target data warehouse or database.

ELT (Extract, Load, Transform)

ELT is an approach that reverses the order of transformation and loading, allowing organizations to load raw data into a target system before performing transformations. Key benefits include:

Faster Data Loading: Raw data can be ingested quickly, making it available for analysis almost immediately.
Flexibility: Organizations can perform transformations as needed, leveraging the processing power of modern data warehouses.

Data Integration Platforms

Data integration platforms provide tools and services for integrating data across various sources. Key features include:

Pre-built Connectors: Many platforms offer connectors for popular applications, databases, and cloud services, simplifying the integration process.
Visual Design Tools: User-friendly interfaces allow users to design integration workflows without extensive coding knowledge.

API-Based Integration

Application Programming Interfaces (APIs) enable systems to communicate and share data seamlessly. Key advantages include:

Real-Time Data Access: APIs facilitate real-time integration, allowing systems to exchange data instantly.
Modularity: API-based integration allows organizations to connect different applications and services, promoting a modular architecture.

Challenges in Data Integration

Despite the importance of data integration, organizations often face several challenges during the process. Understanding these challenges can help in developing effective strategies to address them.

Data Silos

Data silos occur when data is isolated within different departments or systems, preventing seamless integration. Key strategies include:

Cross-Department Collaboration: Encourage collaboration among departments to share data and eliminate silos.
Centralized Data Governance: Establish centralized governance policies to manage data sharing and integration effectively.

Data Quality Issues

Poor data quality can hinder successful integration efforts. Key practices include:

Data Cleansing: Implement data cleansing processes to identify and rectify errors, duplicates, and inconsistencies in the data.

Validation Rules: Establish validation rules to ensure data meets quality standards before integration.

Complex Data Environments

The complexity of modern data environments, including multiple data sources and formats, can complicate integration efforts. Key considerations include:

Data Mapping: Develop comprehensive data mapping strategies to understand how data from different sources correlates and can be integrated.

Scalability: Ensure that integration solutions can scale to accommodate growing data volumes and additional sources over time.

Compliance and Security

Data integration processes must adhere to compliance and security regulations, which can present challenges. Key strategies include:

Regulatory Awareness: Stay informed about relevant data protection regulations that impact data integration efforts.

Access Controls: Implement strict access controls to protect sensitive data during integration processes.

Best Practices for Effective Data Integration

To ensure successful data integration, organizations should follow best practices that promote efficiency and quality. Key practices include:

Define Clear Objectives

Before starting data integration projects, organizations should clearly define their objectives. Key considerations include:

Business Goals: Align integration efforts with overall business goals to ensure they deliver value.
Data Use Cases: Identify specific use cases for integrated data, such as reporting, analytics, or operational efficiency.

Develop a Data Governance Framework

Establishing a data governance framework is essential for managing data quality and compliance during integration. Key elements include:

Data Ownership: Assign data owners responsible for ensuring data quality and integrity throughout the integration process.
Policies and Standards: Develop policies and standards for data handling, quality assurance, and compliance.

Invest in the Right Tools

Selecting appropriate data integration tools can significantly impact the success of integration efforts. Key factors to consider include:

Scalability: Choose tools that can scale to accommodate growing data volumes and diverse sources.
User-Friendliness: Opt for tools with user-friendly interfaces that enable non-technical users to design and manage integration workflows.

Monitor and Optimize Integration Processes

Continuous monitoring and optimization of integration processes are crucial for ensuring ongoing success. Key practices include:

Performance Metrics: Establish key performance indicators (KPIs) to measure the effectiveness and efficiency of data integration.
Feedback Loops: Implement feedback mechanisms to gather input from users and stakeholders, enabling continuous improvement.

Data integration is a vital component of modern data management, enabling organizations to leverage diverse data sources for informed decision-making and operational efficiency. By understanding the various types of data integration, adopting appropriate approaches, and addressing challenges effectively, organizations can create a robust data integration strategy. As the data landscape continues to evolve, maintaining a focus on best practices and continuous improvement will be crucial for maximizing the value of integrated data assets.

Chapter 14: Data Architecture Design

Introduction to Data Architecture

Data architecture is the foundational framework that defines how data is collected, stored, processed, and utilized within an organization. It encompasses the policies, standards, and technologies that govern data management and aims to ensure that data is accessible, reliable, and secure. A well-designed data architecture is crucial for enabling organizations to leverage their data assets effectively, driving business intelligence and analytics initiatives.

Importance of Data Architecture

The importance of data architecture can be underscored through several key aspects:

Alignment with Business Goals: A robust data architecture aligns data management practices with business objectives, ensuring that data supports strategic initiatives.
Scalability and Flexibility: A well-structured architecture allows organizations to scale their data systems efficiently, adapting to changing business needs and technological advancements.

Data Quality and Consistency: Effective architecture incorporates data quality standards, ensuring that data is accurate, consistent, and reliable for decision-making.

Enhanced Data Security: A well-defined architecture includes security measures that protect sensitive data from unauthorized access and breaches.

Key Components of Data Architecture

Data architecture consists of several key components that work together to create a cohesive framework for data management. Understanding these components is essential for effective design and implementation.

Data Sources

Data sources are the origins of data within an organization. They can be categorized as:

Structured Data: Data that is organized in a predefined format, such as relational databases and spreadsheets.

Unstructured Data: Data that does not have a fixed format, including text documents, images, videos, and social media content.

Semi-Structured Data: Data that has some organizational properties but does not fit neatly into tables, such as XML and JSON files.

Data Storage

Data storage refers to the methods and technologies used to store data. Key considerations include:

Databases: Relational databases (e.g., MySQL, PostgreSQL) and NoSQL databases (e.g., MongoDB, Cassandra) serve different use cases based on data structure and access patterns.

Data Lakes: Centralized repositories that store large volumes of raw data in its native format, enabling flexible data exploration and analysis.

Data Warehouses: Specialized storage systems designed for analytical processing, where data is structured and optimized for querying.

Data Integration

Data integration involves combining data from multiple sources to create a unified view. Key integration methods include:

ETL (Extract, Transform, Load): A traditional approach that extracts data from sources, transforms it, and loads it into a target system.

Real-Time Integration: Approaches that enable continuous data flow between systems, ensuring that data is up-to-date and accessible.

API Integration: Utilizing APIs to facilitate data exchange between applications and services.

Data Processing

Data processing refers to the methods used to manipulate and analyze data. Key techniques include:

Batch Processing: Processing large volumes of data at scheduled intervals, often used for historical analysis.
Stream Processing: Real-time processing of data streams, enabling organizations to react to data as it arrives.
Data Analytics: Techniques for analyzing data, including descriptive, predictive, and prescriptive analytics, to derive insights and inform decision-making.

Data Governance

Data governance encompasses the policies and practices that ensure data is managed effectively and ethically. Key elements include:

Data Stewardship: Assigning roles and responsibilities for data management, ensuring accountability and oversight.
Data Quality Standards: Establishing standards and practices to maintain data accuracy, consistency, and reliability.
Compliance and Security: Implementing policies to ensure adherence to regulatory requirements and data protection laws.

Data Architecture Design Principles

When designing a data architecture, several principles should guide the process to ensure it meets organizational needs effectively.

Modularity

A modular architecture allows for the independent development and scaling of components. Key benefits include:

Ease of Maintenance: Changes can be made to individual components without affecting the entire system.
Scalability: Organizations can scale specific modules as needed, accommodating growth in data volume and complexity.

Interoperability

Interoperability ensures that different systems and components can communicate and work together effectively. Key considerations include:

Standardized Interfaces: Utilizing standardized data formats and APIs to facilitate data exchange between systems.
Compatibility: Ensuring that new technologies and components can be integrated with existing systems seamlessly.

Simplicity

Simplicity in data architecture reduces complexity and enhances usability. Key strategies include:

Clear Design: Avoiding overly complicated designs that make it difficult for users to understand and interact with the system.

Minimal Redundancy: Reducing duplication of data and processes to streamline workflows and improve efficiency.

Scalability

A scalable architecture can accommodate growth in data volume and complexity without requiring a complete redesign. Key strategies include:

Cloud Solutions: Leveraging cloud-based technologies that offer elastic scalability, allowing organizations to scale resources up or down as needed.

Distributed Systems: Implementing distributed data storage and processing systems to manage large datasets efficiently.

Security and Compliance

Incorporating security and compliance measures into data architecture is essential for protecting sensitive information. Key considerations include:

Access Controls: Implementing role-based access controls to ensure that only authorized users can access sensitive data.

Data Encryption: Utilizing encryption techniques to protect data at rest and in transit.

Data Architecture Models

Several data architecture models can guide organizations in designing their data management frameworks. Each model offers distinct advantages based on specific use cases and requirements.

Traditional Data Architecture

Traditional data architecture typically involves a centralized model where data is stored in a data warehouse. Key characteristics include:

Structured Data Focus: Primarily focuses on structured data stored in relational databases.
ETL Processes: Relies on ETL processes for data integration, often resulting in batch processing.

Modern Data Architecture

Modern data architecture embraces flexibility and scalability, accommodating both structured and unstructured data. Key features include:

Data Lakes: Utilizes data lakes to store large volumes of raw data, enabling diverse analytics capabilities.
Real-Time Processing: Incorporates real-time data processing capabilities, allowing for immediate insights.

Hybrid Data Architecture

Hybrid data architecture combines on-premises and cloud-based data solutions, offering flexibility and scalability. Key aspects include:

Multi-Cloud Environments: Organizations can utilize multiple cloud providers to optimize costs and performance.
On-Premises Integration: Allows for the integration of on-premises data with cloud services, providing a unified view of data.

Microservices Architecture

Microservices architecture involves breaking down applications into smaller, independent services that can communicate with one another. Key benefits include:

Scalability: Individual services can be scaled independently, allowing for efficient resource allocation.
Agility: Development teams can work on different services concurrently, speeding up the development and deployment process.

Best Practices for Data Architecture Design

To ensure effective data architecture design, organizations should follow best practices that promote efficiency, scalability, and security.

Involve Stakeholders Early

Engaging stakeholders early in the design process is essential for understanding business needs and ensuring alignment. Key activities include:

Requirement Gathering: Conduct workshops and interviews to gather requirements from various stakeholders, including business leaders, IT teams, and end-users.
Feedback Loops: Establish feedback mechanisms to refine the architecture based on stakeholder input throughout the design process.

Emphasize Data Quality

Prioritizing data quality is crucial for ensuring reliable insights and decision-making. Key practices include:

Data Profiling: Conduct data profiling to assess data quality and identify potential issues before integration.
Continuous Monitoring: Implement monitoring processes to continuously assess data quality and address issues as they arise.

Adopt Agile Methodologies

Implementing agile methodologies in data architecture design promotes flexibility and responsiveness to changing needs. Key strategies include:

Iterative Development: Break down architecture design into iterative phases, allowing for gradual implementation and refinement.

Rapid Prototyping: Create prototypes of key components to validate design concepts before full-scale implementation.

Document the Architecture

Thorough documentation of the data architecture is essential for ensuring understanding and guiding future enhancements. Key elements to document include:

Data Flows: Visual representations of data flows within the architecture to illustrate how data moves between components.

Standards and Policies: Clear documentation of data governance standards, security policies, and compliance requirements.

Plan for Future Growth

Considering future growth during the design phase is essential for scalability. Key practices include:

Scalable Technologies: Choose technologies that can scale with growing data volumes and changing business needs.

Future-Proofing: Stay informed about emerging technologies and trends that may impact data architecture and be prepared to adapt as needed.

Data architecture is a fundamental aspect of effective data management, providing the framework for how data is collected, stored, processed, and utilized within an organization. By understanding the key components, principles, and models of data architecture, organizations can design systems that align with their business objectives and support their data-driven initiatives. Emphasizing best practices in design will further enhance the effectiveness, scalability, and security of data architecture, ensuring that organizations can leverage their data assets to drive innovation and competitive advantage.

Chapter 15: Data Security and Privacy

Introduction to Data Security and Privacy

Data security and privacy are critical aspects of modern data management, especially in an era where data breaches and privacy violations are increasingly common. As organizations collect, store, and process vast amounts of sensitive information, they must implement robust security measures and adhere to privacy regulations to protect both their data and their reputation. This chapter explores the concepts of data security and privacy, the various threats organizations face, and the best practices for safeguarding sensitive data.

Importance of Data Security and Privacy

Understanding the importance of data security and privacy is crucial for organizations aiming to protect their assets and maintain customer trust. Key aspects include:

Protection of Sensitive Information: Data security measures help prevent unauthorized access to sensitive information, such as personal identification details, financial records, and health data.

Compliance with Regulations: Many jurisdictions have stringent data protection laws that require organizations to implement specific security measures. Non-compliance can lead to significant fines and legal repercussions.

Trust and Reputation: Customers are increasingly concerned about how their data is handled. A commitment to data security and privacy can enhance brand reputation and foster customer loyalty.

Mitigation of Financial Loss: Data breaches can lead to substantial financial losses due to legal fees, regulatory fines, and the costs associated with remediation efforts. Effective security measures help mitigate these risks.

Types of Data Security Threats

Organizations face various data security threats that can compromise sensitive information. Understanding these threats is essential for developing effective security strategies.

Malware Attacks

Malware, or malicious software, refers to any software designed to harm or exploit systems. Types of malware include:

Viruses: Malicious code that attaches itself to legitimate software and spreads when the infected software is executed.
Ransomware: A type of malware that encrypts files on a victim's system, demanding payment for the decryption key.

Spyware: Software that secretly monitors user activity and collects sensitive information, often without the user's knowledge.

Phishing Attacks

Phishing attacks involve tricking individuals into divulging sensitive information, such as login credentials or financial details. Common tactics include:

Email Phishing: Fraudulent emails that appear to come from legitimate sources, often containing links to fake websites.
Spear Phishing: Targeted phishing attacks aimed at specific individuals or organizations, often using personalized information to increase credibility.

Insider Threats

Insider threats arise from employees or contractors who misuse their access to sensitive data. Key factors include:

Malicious Insiders: Employees who intentionally steal or misuse data for personal gain.
Unintentional Insiders: Employees who inadvertently expose data through careless actions, such as misplacing devices or failing to follow security protocols.

Data Breaches

Data breaches occur when unauthorized individuals gain access to sensitive data. Common causes include:

Hacking: Cybercriminals exploiting vulnerabilities in systems to gain unauthorized access to data.
Physical Theft: Theft of devices containing sensitive data, such as laptops, smartphones, or external drives.

Weak Passwords and Authentication Failures

Weak passwords and inadequate authentication measures can lead to unauthorized access. Key considerations include:

Default Passwords: Many systems come with default passwords that are often not changed, making them easy targets for attackers.
Lack of Multi-Factor Authentication (MFA): Organizations that do not implement MFA increase their risk of unauthorized access, as attackers may gain access using only a compromised password.

Data Privacy Regulations

Data privacy regulations have been established worldwide to protect individuals' personal information and ensure that organizations handle data responsibly. Key regulations include:

General Data Protection Regulation (GDPR)

The GDPR is a comprehensive data protection regulation enacted by the European Union. Key provisions include:

Consent Requirements: Organizations must obtain explicit consent from individuals before collecting or processing their personal data.

Right to Access: Individuals have the right to access their personal data and understand how it is being used.

Right to Erasure: Also known as the "right to be forgotten," individuals can request the deletion of their personal data under certain circumstances.

Health Insurance Portability and Accountability Act (HIPAA)

HIPAA establishes standards for protecting sensitive patient information in the healthcare sector. Key requirements include:

Protected Health Information (PHI): Organizations must implement safeguards to protect PHI from unauthorized access and disclosure.

Breach Notification: In the event of a data breach, organizations must notify affected individuals and the Department of Health and Human Services.

California Consumer Privacy Act (CCPA)

The CCPA enhances privacy rights for California residents. Key provisions include:

Consumer Rights: California residents have the right to know what personal information is being collected and the ability to request deletion of their data.

Opt-Out Option: Organizations must provide consumers with the option to opt-out of the sale of their personal information.

Best Practices for Data Security

To effectively protect sensitive data, organizations should implement best practices for data security. Key practices include:

Implement Strong Access Controls

Access controls are essential for limiting who can access sensitive data. Key strategies include:

Role-Based Access Control (RBAC): Assign access rights based on user roles, ensuring that individuals only have access to data necessary for their job functions.

Regular Access Reviews: Conduct periodic reviews of user access rights to ensure that only authorized individuals can access sensitive data.

Employ Data Encryption

Data encryption protects sensitive information by converting it into an unreadable format. Key considerations include:

Data at Rest: Encrypt sensitive data stored on devices and databases to protect it from unauthorized access.

Data in Transit: Use encryption protocols, such as SSL/TLS, to protect data transmitted over networks.

Regularly Update Software and Systems

Keeping software and systems updated is crucial for protecting against vulnerabilities. Key practices include:

Patch Management: Implement a patch management process to ensure that all software and systems are regularly updated to address known vulnerabilities.

Security Updates: Apply security updates promptly to reduce the risk of exploitation by cybercriminals.

Conduct Employee Training and Awareness

Training employees on data security best practices is essential for minimizing risks. Key activities include:

Security Awareness Programs: Develop training programs that educate employees about common threats, such as phishing and social engineering.

Regular Drills: Conduct regular drills and simulations to reinforce security protocols and ensure employees are prepared to respond to incidents.

Implement Multi-Factor Authentication (MFA)

MFA adds an extra layer of security by requiring users to provide multiple forms of verification before accessing sensitive data. Key considerations include:

Combination of Factors: Implement MFA that requires a combination of something the user knows (password), something they have (security token), and something they are (biometric verification).

Enforcement Across Systems: Apply MFA across all systems that handle sensitive data to enhance overall security.

Best Practices for Data Privacy

In addition to security measures, organizations must implement best practices to protect individual privacy. Key practices include:

Conduct Data Mapping and Inventory

Understanding what data is collected, where it is stored, and how it is processed is crucial for ensuring compliance with privacy regulations. Key activities include:

Data Inventory: Create an inventory of all data assets, including the types of data collected and their sources.

Data Flow Mapping: Document data flows within the organization to identify potential privacy risks and ensure compliance with regulations.

Establish Privacy Policies and Procedures

Clear privacy policies and procedures are essential for guiding data handling practices. Key components include:

Privacy Notices: Provide clear and transparent privacy notices that inform individuals about how their data will be used and their rights under applicable regulations.
Incident Response Plans: Develop and implement incident response plans to address potential data breaches and privacy violations effectively.

Obtain Informed Consent

Organizations must obtain informed consent from individuals before collecting or processing their personal data. Key considerations include:

Clear Language: Use clear and easily understandable language in consent forms, ensuring that individuals understand what they are agreeing to.
Opt-Out Options: Provide individuals with the ability to withdraw their consent at any time and outline the process for doing so.

Regularly Review and Update Privacy Practices

Regular reviews of privacy practices are essential for ensuring ongoing compliance with regulations and addressing emerging risks. Key practices include:

Audits and Assessments: Conduct regular audits and assessments of data handling practices to identify potential compliance gaps.
Stakeholder Feedback: Gather feedback from stakeholders, including customers and employees, to improve privacy practices continuously.

Engage in Vendor Risk Management

Organizations often share sensitive data with third-party vendors, making vendor risk management essential. Key strategies include:

Due Diligence: Conduct thorough due diligence on vendors to assess their data security and privacy practices before engaging them.
Contracts and Agreements: Establish contracts that outline data protection obligations and compliance requirements for third-party vendors.

Data security and privacy are critical components of modern data management, essential for protecting sensitive information and maintaining customer trust. By understanding the various threats organizations face and implementing best practices for both security and privacy, organizations can create a robust framework for safeguarding their data assets. As regulations evolve and data threats continue to increase, organizations must remain vigilant and proactive in their approach to data security and privacy, ensuring they can navigate the complexities of the digital landscape while protecting their stakeholders.

Chapter 16: Performance Optimization Techniques

Introduction to Performance Optimization

Performance optimization is essential for ensuring that databases operate efficiently, providing quick access to data and supporting high-performance applications. In a world where data volumes are continually growing, organizations must employ effective optimization techniques to maintain responsiveness and meet user demands. This chapter delves into various performance optimization strategies for database systems, focusing on key areas such as indexing, query optimization, caching, and hardware considerations.

Importance of Performance Optimization

Optimizing database performance is crucial for several reasons:

User Satisfaction: Fast response times enhance the user experience, leading to higher satisfaction and retention rates.

Resource Efficiency: Optimized databases use fewer resources, reducing costs associated with hardware, cloud services, and energy consumption.

Scalability: Well-optimized databases can handle increased loads more effectively, supporting growth without significant reconfiguration.

Operational Efficiency: Improved performance leads to reduced wait times for queries and transactions, increasing overall productivity.

Understanding Database Performance Metrics

To effectively optimize performance, organizations must first understand key performance metrics that indicate how well a database is functioning. Important metrics include:

Response Time

Response time measures the time taken for a database to respond to a query. It is critical for assessing user experience. Key factors influencing response time include:

Network Latency: The delay in data transmission over the network can impact response times, especially for remote database access.
Query Complexity: More complex queries involving multiple joins and aggregations can take longer to process.

Throughput

Throughput refers to the number of transactions or queries processed by the database within a specific timeframe. High throughput indicates efficient handling of workloads. Factors affecting throughput include:

Concurrent Users: The number of simultaneous users can strain resources, impacting throughput.
Query Optimization: Well-optimized queries are processed faster, improving overall throughput.

Resource Utilization

Monitoring resource utilization helps identify bottlenecks in database performance. Key resources to monitor include:

CPU Usage: High CPU usage can indicate resource contention or inefficient queries.
Memory Usage: Insufficient memory can lead to increased disk I/O, negatively affecting performance.

Disk I/O

Disk I/O measures the read and write operations performed on the disk. High disk I/O can indicate inefficient data access patterns. Key considerations include:

Sequential vs. Random Access: Sequential reads are generally faster than random accesses, so optimizing data storage can improve I/O performance.

Disk Type: The type of storage (e.g., SSDs vs. HDDs) significantly impacts I/O performance, with SSDs typically offering superior speeds.

Techniques for Database Performance Optimization

Various techniques can be employed to optimize database performance effectively. This section explores some of the most effective strategies.

Indexing Strategies

Indexes are critical for improving query performance by allowing the database engine to locate data more efficiently. Key indexing strategies include:

Creating Appropriate Indexes

Selecting the right columns to index can dramatically improve performance. Considerations include:

Primary Keys: Always index primary keys to ensure efficient record retrieval.
Foreign Keys: Index foreign keys to speed up join operations.
Frequently Queried Columns: Identify columns frequently used in WHERE clauses and join conditions for indexing.

b. Index Maintenance

Regularly maintaining indexes is essential to ensure they remain effective. Key practices include:

Rebuilding and Reorganizing: Periodically rebuild or reorganize fragmented indexes to optimize storage and retrieval efficiency.

Monitoring Usage: Track index usage to identify unused or rarely used indexes that may need to be removed to reduce overhead.

Query Optimization

Optimizing queries can lead to significant performance improvements. Key strategies include:

Analyzing Query Plans

Most database management systems provide tools to analyze query execution plans. By examining these plans, you can identify inefficiencies. Key aspects to analyze include:

Join Types: Understand the types of joins used and their implications on performance.

Scan vs. Seek: Identify whether the query is performing a full table scan or a more efficient index seek.

b. Refactoring Queries

Simplifying and restructuring queries can enhance performance. Key practices include:

Avoiding SELECT *: Instead of selecting all columns, specify only the necessary columns to reduce data transfer.
Using Subqueries Wisely: Consider whether subqueries can be replaced with joins or vice versa, based on performance analysis.

Caching Strategies

Caching is a powerful technique for improving database performance by reducing the need for repeated data retrieval from disk. Key caching strategies include:

In-Memory Caching

Utilizing in-memory caches, such as Redis or Memcached, can drastically reduce access times for frequently accessed data. Key considerations include:

Cache Expiry: Set appropriate cache expiry times to balance freshness and performance.
Cache Size: Allocate sufficient memory for caching to ensure that the most frequently accessed data is stored.

b. Query Result Caching

Some database systems offer query result caching, storing the results of frequently executed queries for faster retrieval. Key considerations include:

Cache Invalidation: Implement mechanisms to invalidate cache entries when underlying data changes to ensure data accuracy.
Configuration: Tune caching parameters based on usage patterns to optimize performance.

Partitioning and Sharding

Partitioning and sharding are techniques used to divide data into smaller, manageable segments, enhancing performance and scalability.

Data Partitioning

Partitioning involves dividing large tables into smaller, more manageable pieces based on certain criteria (e.g., range, list, or hash). Key benefits include:

Improved Query Performance: Queries can be executed against smaller partitions, reducing the amount of data scanned.
Easier Maintenance: Managing smaller partitions is often simpler than handling a single large table.

b. Data Sharding

Sharding involves distributing data across multiple database instances or servers. Key advantages include:

Horizontal Scalability: Sharding allows organizations to scale out their database infrastructure by adding more servers.

Load Balancing: Distributing data across multiple servers can help balance load and reduce contention.

Hardware and Infrastructure Considerations

While software optimization is essential, hardware and infrastructure also play a critical role in database performance. Key considerations include:

Choosing the Right Storage

The choice of storage can significantly impact database performance. Key options include:

Solid-State Drives (SSDs): SSDs provide faster read and write speeds compared to traditional hard disk drives (HDDs), enhancing overall performance.
RAID Configurations: Implementing RAID configurations can improve redundancy and performance by distributing data across multiple disks.

b. Scaling Resources

As data volumes grow, organizations must ensure that their hardware resources can keep pace. Key strategies include:

Vertical Scaling: Increasing the capacity of existing hardware (e.g., adding RAM or CPU power) can enhance performance.
Horizontal Scaling: Adding additional servers to distribute the load can improve performance and resilience.

Monitoring and Performance Tuning

Continuous monitoring is essential for maintaining optimal database performance. Key practices include:

Utilizing Performance Monitoring Tools

Investing in performance monitoring tools can provide insights into database health and performance. Key benefits include:

Real-Time Monitoring: Continuous monitoring allows for immediate identification of performance issues.
Historical Analysis: Analyzing historical performance data can reveal trends and help identify areas for improvement.

b. Setting Performance Baselines

Establishing performance baselines enables organizations to track improvements over time and identify deviations from expected performance. Key practices include:

Regular Assessments: Conduct performance assessments at regular intervals to ensure that databases are meeting established baselines.
Adjusting Configurations: Use insights gained from performance monitoring to adjust database configurations and resource allocations as needed.

Performance optimization is a critical aspect of effective database management, enabling organizations to provide fast and responsive access to data. By employing a variety of techniques—ranging from indexing and query optimization to caching and infrastructure enhancements—organizations can significantly improve database performance. Continuous monitoring and adjustment are essential to maintain optimal performance in the face of evolving workloads and data volumes. As organizations increasingly rely on data-driven decision-making, optimizing database performance will play a vital role in achieving their strategic objectives.

Chapter 17: Future Trends in Database Management

Introduction to Future Trends

As technology continues to evolve at a rapid pace, the field of database management is undergoing significant transformations. New trends, driven by advancements in computing, data analytics, and user expectations, are reshaping how databases are designed, deployed, and managed. This chapter explores the future trends in database management, focusing on the implications of cloud computing, artificial intelligence, NoSQL databases, data privacy and security, and the impact of emerging technologies.

The Shift to Cloud-Based Database Solutions

The adoption of cloud computing has revolutionized the landscape of database management. Organizations are increasingly moving their database systems to cloud platforms due to numerous benefits.

Scalability and Flexibility

Cloud-based databases offer unparalleled scalability, allowing organizations to quickly adjust resources based on demand. This elasticity is particularly beneficial for applications with fluctuating workloads, such as e-commerce platforms during peak shopping seasons.

Elastic Provisioning: Cloud providers offer elastic provisioning, allowing organizations to scale up or down based on real-time requirements without significant upfront investments.

Global Reach: Cloud databases can be deployed in multiple geographic regions, improving latency and performance for users worldwide.

Cost Efficiency

The pay-as-you-go model of cloud services can lead to substantial cost savings for organizations.

Reduced Capital Expenditures: Organizations can avoid significant capital expenditures on hardware and software by leveraging cloud services.

Operational Efficiency: The maintenance of hardware and software is managed by cloud providers, allowing organizations to focus on core business activities.

Managed Services

Many cloud providers offer managed database services, reducing the burden of database administration.

Automatic Backups and Updates: Managed services handle routine tasks such as backups, updates, and patch management, ensuring that databases are always up to date and secure.

Performance Monitoring: Cloud providers often offer built-in monitoring tools that help organizations track database performance and optimize usage.

The Rise of NoSQL Databases

The traditional relational database model is being challenged by NoSQL databases, which are designed to handle unstructured and semi-structured data more effectively.

Variety of Data Models

NoSQL databases support various data models, including document, key-value, column-family, and graph databases. This flexibility allows organizations to choose the most suitable model for their specific use cases.

Document Stores: Databases like MongoDB allow for the storage of complex data structures as documents, making them ideal for applications requiring rich data representations.

Graph Databases: Technologies like Neo4j are increasingly used for applications that involve complex relationships, such as social networks and recommendation engines.

High Performance and Scalability

NoSQL databases are built to handle large volumes of data and high-velocity transactions, making them suitable for modern applications.

Distributed Architecture: Many NoSQL databases utilize a distributed architecture, enabling horizontal scaling and improved performance under heavy loads.

Eventual Consistency: Unlike traditional databases that prioritize immediate consistency, NoSQL databases often embrace eventual consistency, allowing for faster write operations.

Integration of Artificial Intelligence and Machine Learning

The integration of AI and machine learning into database management is poised to transform how organizations interact with their data.

Automated Database Management

AI-driven automation is streamlining database management tasks, reducing the need for manual intervention.

Intelligent Query Optimization: AI algorithms can analyze query patterns and optimize execution plans in real-time, improving performance without human input.

Predictive Maintenance: Machine learning models can predict potential failures or performance degradation, allowing for proactive maintenance and minimizing downtime.

Enhanced Data Insights

AI and machine learning facilitate deeper data analysis, enabling organizations to extract valuable insights from their data.

Automated Data Classification: AI can automate the classification of data, making it easier to manage and retrieve information based on context.

Anomaly Detection: Machine learning algorithms can identify unusual patterns in data, helping organizations detect potential fraud or security breaches.

Data Privacy and Security Concerns

As data regulations tighten globally, organizations must prioritize data privacy and security in their database management strategies.

Compliance with Regulations

The introduction of regulations like GDPR and CCPA mandates that organizations implement strict data protection measures.

Data Governance Frameworks: Organizations are adopting data governance frameworks to ensure compliance with regulations and manage data effectively.

Privacy by Design: Incorporating privacy considerations into the design and architecture of database systems is becoming a standard practice.

Enhanced Security Measures

The evolving threat landscape necessitates more robust security measures for database management.

Zero Trust Architecture: Many organizations are adopting a zero trust approach, which assumes that threats can exist both inside and outside the network, requiring strict verification for every user and device.

Advanced Encryption Techniques: Organizations are increasingly utilizing advanced encryption methods to protect sensitive data both at rest and in transit.

The Impact of Emerging Technologies

Emerging technologies such as blockchain, edge computing, and the Internet of Things (IoT) are influencing database management practices.

Blockchain Technology

Blockchain technology offers a decentralized and secure way to manage data, particularly for applications requiring transparency and immutability.

Distributed Ledger Systems: Blockchain databases can provide a secure and transparent record of transactions, making them suitable for industries like finance and supply chain management.

Smart Contracts: Automated smart contracts can enhance transaction efficiency and reduce the need for intermediaries.

Edge Computing

Edge computing shifts data processing closer to the source of data generation, reducing latency and bandwidth usage.

Real-Time Data Processing: Databases deployed at the edge can process data in real-time, which is critical for applications like autonomous vehicles and industrial IoT.

Reduced Data Transfer Costs: By processing data locally, organizations can minimize the amount of data sent to centralized data centers, reducing costs and improving response times.

The Evolution of Database Management Systems

The future of database management systems (DBMS) will likely see significant innovations that cater to evolving user needs.

Hybrid and Multi-Cloud Solutions

Organizations are increasingly adopting hybrid and multi-cloud strategies, allowing them to leverage the strengths of different cloud providers and on-premises infrastructure.

Flexibility and Redundancy: Hybrid solutions provide flexibility in data deployment while ensuring redundancy and disaster recovery options.

Cost Optimization: Multi-cloud strategies allow organizations to optimize costs by selecting the most cost-effective services for specific workloads.

Serverless Architectures

Serverless computing allows organizations to focus on application development without worrying about managing servers.

Dynamic Resource Allocation: Serverless architectures automatically allocate resources based on demand, optimizing performance and cost.

Faster Development Cycles: By abstracting infrastructure management, developers can focus on building applications and deploying features more rapidly.

The future of database management is marked by rapid advancements and transformative trends that are reshaping how organizations manage their data. The shift to cloud-based solutions, the rise of NoSQL databases, the integration of AI and machine learning, the emphasis on data privacy and security, and the influence of emerging technologies are all critical factors shaping this landscape. As organizations navigate these changes, adopting innovative approaches to database management will be essential for maintaining competitive advantages and effectively leveraging data in an increasingly complex digital world.

www.ingramcontent.com/pod-product-compliance
Lightning Source LLC
Chambersburg PA
CBHW071456220526
45472CB00003B/824